GUIDE
TO A GOOD
MARRIAGE

Life Changing Lessons for Christian Men to Build the Marriage You Want

DR. DAN MCKAY

Guide to a Good Marriage by Dr. Dan McKay

Published by Creative Ideas Publishing

For permissions contact:

permissions@creativeideaspublishing.com

ISBN: 978-1-952016-39-4

Lovingly Dedicated

...To my precious wife Joyce

Thank you for loving me.

...To our children

Jeremy and Rachel

Aaron and Amy

Carrie and Daniel

Seth and Autumn

Thank you for the privilege of being your dad.

...To a group of young couples who Joyce and I shared our life with each week for many years. I was titled their Bible teacher, but in many ways, they taught me. These couples were a source of fun, insight, and inspiration.

Jonathan and Kora, Robby and Cathy, Earl and Erica, David and Jonell, Jason C. and Ashley, Darren and Jeannie, Craig and Carina, Christina and Troy, Todd and Kristin, Chad and Lauren, Kevin and Leslie, Aaron and Cami, Jordan and Dana, Josh and Chelsea, Wes and Amy, Eric and Angie, Clint and Amy, Lewis and Rachel, Jason R. and Ashley, Chad and Mindy, Nate and Maria, John and Jenelle, Michael and Laurie, Tim and Tyra, Kenny and Donna, Jonathan and Amanda, Mike and Erin, Scott and Tamara, Stan and Angela, Lee and Amanda, Wade and Breanna, Cody and Lindsey, Cory and Hailee, Bart and Jennifer, Danny and Katrina, Howard and Erin, David and Gail, Robbie and Carla, Scott S. and Kim, Grant and Lindsey, Greg and Mary Jane, Scott E. and Melissa, and Wallace and Ann.

Thank you for your love and faithfulness to Christ, and in His love, caring for Joyce and me.

GUIDE TO A **GOOD MARRIAGE**

Contents

GUIDE TO A **GOOD MARRIAGE**

Introduction
I Can Help

I am sure I can help.

Whether you are looking for "helpful hints" to improve your marriage, the motivation and inspiration to do better as a husband, or affirmation that you are on target as a husband . . . I can help.

For over 30 years, I have listened to couples who have found a way to make each other miserable. I don't believe it was their plan or intent; however, sadly it happened. Most couples I have counseled had a moment of "blue sky and sunshine" when they pledged their love "For Better or Worse," believing each day in the future would be better. I have counseled numerous couples who believed their wedding day was entry into the fairy tale realm of "happily ever after." Unfortunately, in the weeks that followed they did not find better, or "happily ever after," they only found "the worse."

But let me share some great news . . . there is still time for "better" in your marriage.

WHERE ARE YOU?

Maybe you are just beginning your journey of marriage. If so, I am excited for you and the possibilities that are before you and your wife. Marriage is a wonderful gift, and I believe the words in this book will help you care for it.

Some of you may be wondering if your marriage is beyond repair. However, if you are reading these words, you have not given up hope . . . and I am glad. The fact is, there is reason for hope. I believe a better marriage, one that is satisfying for both you and your wife is possible, and sooner than you might think.

Presently, you might believe your "marriage story" is different from anyone else's marriage and that your marriage is the "worse" marriage on the face of planet Earth. However, let me be clear. Somewhere in the past, there was a husband who sat in my office and shared "your" story.... only to find the way back into his wife's heart (or allow his wife back into his heart). Consequently, if you take the time to read the following pages there is "a word" for you that will help you have a stronger marriage.

Whatever your circumstances (newlywed or seasoned warrior), I am proud of you for taking the time to be intentional about your marriage.

Here is some additional Good News. A Good Marriage is Easier than a Bad Marriage.

True, a good marriage is not an accident. It does not happen without effort. However, a bad marriage is exhausting and will drain every ounce of energy out of your body. A bad marriage will bring dismal days and sleepless nights, whereas a good marriage has the potential of breathing life into your day. I love the passage in Joshua where Joshua proclaims to the people, "Choose this day whom you will serve...but as for me and my house we will serve the Lord" (Joshua 24:15; ESV). Joshua made a great choice. Today, I would encourage you to make a similar proclamation regarding your marriage. This day, take out your calendar, circle today's date, and proclaim, "From this day on, for me and my family, I choose a good marriage."

ABOUT ME

I love helping couples. For over 25 years, I have spoken at marriage enrichment conferences across the country with my lovely wife, Joyce (of 42 years). Thirty eight years I served as one of the pastors at a wonderful church, "doing life" and "loving on" a tremendous community of God's children.

I have been blessed with teachers, mentors and friends who comprise some of the most outstanding and renown counselors in this country (Dr. Doug Rosenau, Dr. Ed Worthington, Dr. Gary Oliver, Dr. Mark Laaser,

I Can Help 3

Dr. Fred DiBlasio). I have a doctorate in marriage and family counseling. Serving as a pastoral care minister, I have had the honor of entwining my life with countless families as they experienced the joy and struggles of life, and I have counseled married couples for over 38 years. During these years, it has been my privilege to help many couples find their way to successful and healthy marriages.

I love my family. Joyce and I were blessed with four awesome children who through marriage brought us four more wonderful children (Jeremy and Rachel, Aaron and Amy, Carrie Anne and Daniel, Seth and Autumn). In addition, we have 9 precious grandchildren (Foster, Maddox, Peter, Easton, Georgia, Payson, Molly Dot, Daniel, and Fox).

MARRIAGE: A DESTINATION ON THE MAP

There is no reason to make the path to a good marriage complicated. It is not an unattainable goal. It is not beyond your reach. However, it will not happen without your intentional involvement. Allow me to be your guide and this book a map.

Now I realize that a lot of guys do not need a map. Men often live on the edge of adventure attempting "to boldly go where no man has gone before." However, many a wise man has discovered the value of a map. A map can point out places of interest you don't want to miss as you travel. A map can also help you identify "dead ends" or obstacles that will hinder your journey. Consequently, there are times a map is an extremely helpful item to have in your possession, especially when your map has a location on it you desire to travel.

If the destination you are seeking is a good marriage, the following pages will offer you a guide to help you on your journey.

GUIDE TO A **GOOD MARRIAGE**

Chapter 1
Be Nice

I met Ryan in the parking lot at McDonald's. He jokingly told me his Happy Meal was not as happy as he had hoped it would be. Unfortunately, minutes before this lighthearted statement, I found Ryan in his car weeping and grasping his steering wheel as if gravity had failed and it was the only thing holding him to earth. Even for me, it was emotionally difficult to see such a strong young man so broken. Sadly, his next statement was one I have heard too often from young men and women. Starting to break down again, Ryan said, "Erica said she is done with us! She said she will always love me, but she is not 'in love' with me... whatever that means."

When I asked Ryan what happened, he explained that as he arrived home from work Erica met him at the door and asked him to take out the trash.

Ryan said he responded by telling her he would do it later, after which Erica "just exploded," telling him she was "done" and to get out of the house. When he called her from McDonald's to see if she had calmed down, Erica told him, as Ryan put it, "that stuff about her loving me but not being 'in love' with me."

Red faced and perplexed, Ryan exclaimed, "I just don't understand!"

I often meet wonderful couples - a really great guy and an awesome young lady, who are struggling because of the impact of one word carelessly spoken, or one action hastily performed, but it should not be that way. When one action or ill-advised word can capsize a relationship, it is rarely the real issue. Typically, this involves a husband and wife who have forgotten the importance of "Being Nice." With the couple failing to properly care for one another, resentment begins to build, and feelings of neglect take root. The relationship now becomes vulnerable to the point where a "certain look" or "word" perceived negatively, results in a firestorm of emotions.

It is very important that you and I, "Be Nice!"

You might be thinking, "You have got to be kidding!" or "I can't believe I paid money to hear the same advice my mom gave me in middle school." Before you stop reading, please know that these two words "Be Nice" are extremely critical.

If I were to ask you if you put gas in your car, you might be offended by the simplicity of the question. We both know it takes fuel for an engine to run. However, when I was 16 years old, my car ran out of gas and I ended up coasting under a bridge on Interstate 75 in Atlanta. In a hurry to arrive at my destination, I was overly confident I could drive on empty. Optimism (or neglect) did not take me where I needed to go. Without fuel, you and I will eventually be sitting in our cars on the side of the road extremely frustrated.

"Being Nice" to your wife is like putting gas in a car. Being nice is fuel for your marriage relationship. If your marriage is running on fumes, don't take your marriage for granted assuming you will arrive at some wonderful destination as a couple. It will not happen.

When I spoke with Erica later that evening, she claimed that Ryan was the one who had given up on the marriage. Contained in her long list of grievances regarding his negligence of her, she included such statements as:

- He never helps out around the house, unless he wants sex.
- He usually comes home from work in a bad mood, and then sits in front of the TV for the remainder of the evening.
- He typically responds to her with grunts instead of words.
- He seldom offers to help with the children.

Be Nice 9

- He treats strangers nicer than he treats her.
- He never shows her any attention, unless he wants sex.

Ryan is a great guy, and anyone who knows Ryan could give Erica a list of reasons why Erica is fortunate to have him in her life, but even Ryan was quick to admit he had taken Erica for granted for a long time. (In reality, it is a common occurrence for most of us at some point.) However, Ryan was now ready to walk on burning hot coals if Erica would give him a chance to prove his love for her. It was time for Ryan to wake up and "Be Nice." (Thankfully in the days ahead, Erica gave Ryan the time and space to prove the sincerity of his words.)

On the day of my daughter's wedding, minutes before escorting her down the aisle to "give her away," she asked if I had any advice for her and her fiancé Daniel. There was no time for a long diatribe on marriage. I simply said, "Carrie Anne, if you can continue to BE NICE to Daniel, you will have a great marriage." These were not callous words, or careless rhetoric from a task driven Dad who was overly focused on the "presenting problem" of walking his precious daughter down the aisle. I deeply believed what I said.

For many years I have encouraged couples with these two simple words "Be Nice." During these years, I have seen the tremendous difference it makes in the lives of couples who take seriously the value of implementing a "Be Nice" strategy in their marriage. It may sound trivial, but these two words, "Be Nice" can make a significant difference in your life and in your marriage.

Even though "Being Nice" can be descriptive of a specific event, it is my hope that you will consider adopting it as a lifestyle. As a husband who is "Being Nice," you are living your life with intentional moments through which, by word and deed, you are attempting to express kindness to your wife. In doing so, you are not only fueling (nurturing) your marriage relationship, but you are also living your life in obedience to God's Word.

BEING NICE IS A SPIRITUAL ACT

Few of us would debate the value of food, or sleep. If we neglect either, it significantly compromises our ability to function. No doubt, you have heard cautionary statements about the danger of engaging your wife in discussing conflictual issues when either of you are either tired (and needing sleep) or hungry (needing food). Truly, debating important issues when we are hungry is typically a recipe for an ugly fight, a poor decision, and a bad taste in your mouth. In the same way, trying to convince your wife to engage in a sexual encounter when she is sleepy is a trip down Futility Avenue (and that is a treacherous road for any husband).

Just as you and I need food and sleep, we need to Be Nice. This may sound as if I am exaggerating, but I believe Being Nice helps nourish our souls. Being Nice is Soul Food. Being Nice is a fulfillment of our created purpose. God's Word tells us, "For we are His workmanship, created in Christ Jesus for good works, which God prepared beforehand so that we would walk in them" (Ephesians 2:10). Galatians 6:9 proclaims, "Be kind to one another, tenderhearted, forgiving one another, as God in Christ forgave you." God made you to Be Nice.

Being Nice is Soul Food

As a husband, your primary expression of good works should be lived out as you express love to your wife,... as you are nice to her. You might not have recognized it in the past, but when you are nice to your wife, you are fulfilling God's claim on your life. You are doing a spiritual work. Scripture proclaims this clearly, "Husbands, love your wives as Christ loved the church and gave himself up for her" (Ephesians 5:25).

I love the way Ephesians 4 lays claim to our lives. In verse 1 we are reminded to "Live worthy of the calling you have received." As a Christian husband, God's Word calls you to live a worthy life. As husbands, we should be living a life of meaning and significance, which by the choices we make, is honoring to our Lord. In the final verse of chapter 4, the verse states, "Be

Kind..." (verse 32). These verses remind us that as a husband we need to live worthy and we need to be nice. This is truly an Awesome Call on your life:

Live Worthy . . . Be Kind

DO NOT DISREGARD

As mentioned, it would be easy to discount these two words "Be Nice," as so simple or basic that we fail to see the importance of them. Granted, it is quite easy to say, "BE NICE," not so easy to do. Sadly, I often deal with couples who are blind to the value of being nice. In fact, I believe the majority of husbands and wives struggle with being nice to one another.

Regrettably, there are numerous husbands and wives who believe marriage entitles them to bring the worst of who they are and dump it on their mate. It is as if they believe marriage is a safe zone to treat one's husband or wife in any hurtful way desired. I hope you know this is horribly wrong. Marriage is not the freedom to treat a married partner carelessly. It is not a license to demean, degrade, or belittle.

Marriage carries with it the responsibility to love. It carries the RESPONSIBILITY TO BE NICE.

YOUR WIFE - YOUR PRIORITY

From the moment a couple marries, one of the primary concerns for the husband should be the health and well-being of his wife. God's Word makes this abundantly clear. In Genesis 2:24 we read, "Therefore a man shall leave his father and mother and be joined to his wife, and they shall become one flesh." Jesus echoes these words in Matthew 19:5, "For this reason, a man shall leave his father and mother and be joined to his wife, and the two shall become one flesh."

In reading these passages, don't miss the importance of them. In the patriarchal system of the day, it was not the man who left his father and mother, it was the woman. The woman would leave her family and "move in" with her new husband and his family.

If the woman was the one who left her family, why does Jesus say, "For this reason a man shall leave his father and mother and be joined to his wife"? Was Jesus redefining the customs of the day? Was Jesus telling us he wanted the man to leave his family and move in with his wife's mom and dad? No, that was not His point.

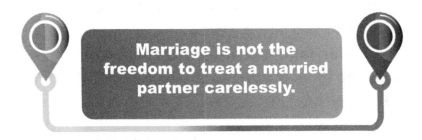

Marriage is not the freedom to treat a married partner carelessly.

I believe Jesus' words are proclaiming the priority of the wife in the husband's life. From the time a man marries a woman, he reprioritizes his life. Neither mom nor dad, best friend from college, nor his favorite hunting dog is more important than his wife. The husband is to leave his mom and dad and is now to "be joined" with his wife. His mom and dad are still important, but his wife is now his priority. In a time when Jewish rabbis were proclaiming a husband could leave his wife if she burnt his food or if the husband found a woman more beautiful; Jesus was affirming the priority of marriage and the priority of the wife.

Let me be clear: In all the known world, no one has the responsibility to care for your wife as you do. It is not her gal pals, your neighbor, or her male co-worker who has the responsibility to encourage her or show her kindness. It is you! You are to help her see herself as Jesus sees her --- A precious treasure that He would give His life to save.

Your first Responsibility (with respect to human relationships) is to care for your wife.

YOU ARE THE MAN!

You serve a magnificent and significant role in the well-being of your wife. As you are "Being Nice" the question you must ask yourself is, "What is my wife's condition?" Another question of utmost importance is, "What is my wife's condition after an encounter with me?... Does my wife feel encouraged? After spending time with me, does my wife feel valued?"

I am not trying to place the success of the marriage on your shoulders. However, I am asking you to recognize the important role you serve in your wife's life. A positive self-image and feelings of significance for the wife are nurtured in a marriage where the husband takes the simple step of "being nice" to his wife.

With this truth, I hope you can also acknowledge what occurs when the husband is Not Nice to his wife. When a husband fails to "Be Nice," feelings of neglect can potentially take root in his wife's heart and mind. These feelings will undermine the marriage relationship. In this setting a wife may feel devalued, which can lead to her distancing herself from her husband.

If you want your wife to be drawn to you,if you desire her to "want to be with you," be nice.

A HEALTHY EXERCISE

1. Whenever possible and as much as possible, become an active observer and student of your interactions with your wife. (Evaluate how you handle your encounters with her. Would your words towards her be defined by others as words of kindness? Can your actions be labeled with our guiding principle of "Being Nice"?)

2. Begin purging your life of words and actions which are not appropriate. Put on trial for "Being Nice" to your wife, there should be conclusive evidence that would guarantee a conviction.

A MENTAL REMINDER

The fuel gauge on my car is a helpful reminder of my car's need for gas. My car even has a warning light that blinks the message "low fuel," when my tank is extremely low. It would be wonderful if we each had a gauge that displayed the health of our marriage. It could help us realize our need to "fuel" our marriage relationship in those times when the tank is almost empty. In the absence of a gauge, I would encourage you to use each time you look at your gas gauge or fill your car's tank with gas as a simple reminder of your need to "Be Nice" to your wife.

You may want to go out to your car right now and check your fuel gauge.

Guess What, It Is Time To Be Nice!

Please Note: Except for the chapter entitled "Got Game," the names of individuals mentioned in this book have been changed to protect their privacy.

GUIDE TO A **GOOD MARRIAGE**

Chapter 2
Expectations & Neutral Encounters

As I walked down the hallway at church, I noticed Lynn and Beth speaking with one another. It was evident from Lynn's facial expressions and hand gestures that she and Beth were involved in a very intense conversation. Approaching them, I heard Lynn exclaim, "I just wish he would hold my hand like he used to!"

I don't typically intrude into someone's conversation, but I had officiated at Lynn's wedding and I felt a special responsibility for her marital well-being. Disappointingly, Lynn proceeded to tell me that her husband Jack was not doing the "affectionate acts" he did early in their marriage. Lynn explained, "He doesn't hold my hand like he used to. He seldom hugs me. In fact, he hardly does anything to show me physical affection."

When I asked Lynn if she had talked to Jack, she said she had, but the conversation went poorly. In response to her concerns, Lynn said Jack defended his lack of affection by saying, "That's just not me, I am just not that way."

I hope you realize that Jack's rationale for not being affectionate is unacceptable. Can you imagine Jack being at work and using the same response with his boss? Picture Jack going to work on Monday morning and his boss asking him to do something, and Jack responding, "Gee Boss, I would love to help, but that task is just not me. It is just not who I am." If Jack gave that response to his boss, Jack would probably be boxing up his personal items from his office and looking for another job on Tuesday.

Is it fair or reasonable for Jack to use a certain response with Lynn, that he would never consider using with his boss? No, it is not!

Truly, as a husband the issue is never "Who you are."

The Real Issue is: Who are you Willing "To Be," And What are you Willing "To Do" To Ensure your Wife feels Loved?

Love is experienced in a variety of ways. I have had young ladies tell me they feel sexually stimulated when they see their husbands vacuuming the house. However, I believe personal interactions (word and touch), between a husband and wife are at a different level. Expectations around the home are important and we will address those in this chapter. Nonetheless, of critical importance is the manner you care for your wife with kind word and gentle embrace.

Whereas some expectations in a marriage may be negotiable, expectations regarding affection and Lynn's sense of feeling loved should never be viewed as negotiable. If Lynn expects her husband to hug her and hold her hand, Jack needs to "step up," fulfill those expectations and "Be the Man." Jack is the only man in

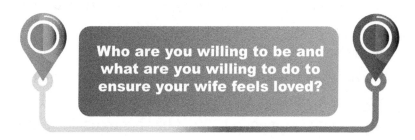

Who are you willing to be and what are you willing to do to ensure your wife feels loved?

Lynn's life that is to fulfill those needs. Someone else can paint the bedroom, clean the house, cut the grass, change the oil in her car, ... etc. Only Jack should hold her hand in companionship. If Jack fails to fulfill that responsibility, there "should be" no one else to do it.

ASSIGNMENT

Step One: Ask your wife to respond to the following statement: I feel loved when ...

Step Two: Do it!

Expectations & Neutral Encounters

Commentary: Unlike Ryan and Erica from chapter one, Jack and Lynn's story was not as pleasant. If Jack had awakened to Lynn's need for physical affection, the relationship would have undoubtedly improved. Unfortunately, Jack continued to hide behind his belief that "Who He Is" was an adequate defense to "NOT BE" who Lynn needed. Truly, as a Christian husband it is not "your rights" that you should focus on, but "your responsibility" to love your wife.

Do you know the old hymn entitled "Just As I Am"? The song refers to our coming to Jesus, who accepts us "Just As We Are," in spite of the fact we are such a mess. In Jack's version of "Just As I Am," he emphasized he was coming to Lynn Just As He Was, and he was not about to change. It is a wise man who is faithful to his wife instead of faithful to some preconceived idea that he is "weak" or "less of a man" if he is not true to himself. Lynn was crying out to Jack, saying she needed someone to "hold her hand" as Jack continually hid behind his excuse of "I Am Just Not that way. It is Just Not who I Am."

Have you ever had a small crack in your car's windshield that you planned on repairing? Preoccupied with life, you fail to act, hoping the crack will not worsen. Unfortunately, to your dismay, one morning you walk out to your car and discover the crack has spread across the windshield.

Sadly, the crack that Jack allowed in his marriage spread to the point it made it difficult for Lynn to clearly see her responsibility to be faithful to Jack. Desiring someone to hold her hand, she met someone at work who claimed he yearned for that opportunity. What Lynn did was horribly wrong. She allowed Jack's failure to her, to justify her unfaithfulness to him. However, both Jack and Lynn share in the responsibility for the failure of their marriage.

I pray that you will never allow pride, or the desire to be right, or claims of "your rights," to interfere with your ability and your responsibility to love your wife. Remember, you are God's representative in loving her!

EXPECTATIONS AND NEUTRAL ENCOUNTERS

The expectations that a husband and wife have of one another have a direct correlation to the sense of satisfaction felt by the couple. Expectations will also impact what actions are interpreted as "Acts of Kindness" in the marriage.

If you grew up in a home where your mom cooked, cleaned the home, and massaged your dad's feet every Friday evening, there is a strong likelihood that on Friday night you are taking your socks off, propping your feet on a foot stool, and expecting a foot massage from your wife. (If your wife's home was one where her dad did the laundry, it could explain why you have no clean clothes.)

Clarifying expectations in a marriage is a point of stress and disappointment for many husbands. However, in our desire to Be Nice to our wives, it is important that a husband clearly understand his wife's expectations.

Many husbands will find that a considerable number of their encounters with their wives are Neutral Encounters. A husband may attempt to label these Neutral Encounters as actions where he is being a good or "nice" husband, but there is a strong likelihood that the husband's actions are not viewed in that manner by his wife. In his wife's mind, he is simply maintaining the "status quo" or doing his part.

LET ME EXPLAIN NEUTRAL ENCOUNTERS

A Neutral Encounter is an interaction between a husband and wife in which there is No Inherent Niceness Quotient. As noted, this can even be an action where the husband performs functional tasks within the home, which he defines as "Nice," but they are not perceived in that manner by the wife. This usually occurs when certain roles the husband performs are viewed by his wife as "his responsibility." The husband is completing tasks the wife EXPECTS HIM TO COMPLETE. He is fulfilling her expectations of him as her husband. (I realize we could debate the issue of a "neutral act," with someone claiming that no act is ever neutral. However, I would ask that you at least accept the premise that certain acts of service you perform around the house might not have the positive effect on your wife for which you were hoping.) Merely meeting expectations will not increase your Niceness Quotient. Exceeding expectations will be required.

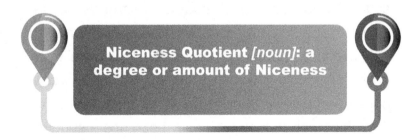

Niceness Quotient *[noun]*: a degree or amount of Niceness

Potential Neutral Encounters

> **The Wife States:** The oil light came on in the car.
> **The Husband's Reply:** I will take it by Jiffy Lube in the morning.

> **The Wife Asks:** Did you take out the trash?
> **The Husband's Reply:** No, the trashcan still had some room in it.

> **The Wife Asks:** Isn't this your day to pick up the children?
> **The Husband's Reply:** Yes, but presently my foot is wedged in the trashcan.

THE FALLACY OF THE 50/50 MARRIAGE

I have officiated the marriages for hundreds of couples and prior to marriage I have heard numerous young couples state, "We plan on sharing everything 50/50." However, in the efficiency of maintaining a home, it is common that the husband begins performing certain tasks, while the wife assumes other specific responsibilities. The concept of "we are doing everything together" sounds great, but it is cumbersome to enact. It is an impractical policy for most businesses and difficult to maintain in the home. Consequently, if a wife believes it is her husband's "job" to take out the trash, this act will not be perceived by her as an act of kindness. In fact, if he does not do it, it potentially becomes a source of irritation for the wife.

When fixed roles have become established in the marriage, there can be numerous "neutral encounters." Thus, in performing the task the husband is fulfilling his responsibility. He is doing "his part." Completion of the task is not "Being Nice," it is the husband "shouldering his share of the load." Being Nice requires a husband do more than fulfill tasks needed to maintain the home. It is great when a man does his part in fulfilling household tasks. However, if the majority of interactions with your wife are Neutral Encounters, it is time to add "Being Nice" to your day.

A HEALTHY EXERCISE

1. Make a list of the expectations you and your wife have of one another as it pertains to maintaining your home.
2. Ask your wife to prepare a similar list as in step 1.
3. As a matter of clarification, review the list with your wife.

4. Reflect on the list of expectations your wife has of you. Select one of her expectations and think of some action you can "add to" her expectation, that would create an act of "Being Nice." For example, your wife expects you to load the dishwasher every evening and unload it in the morning. After unloading the dishwasher one morning, "to be nice" you put a plate on the counter and place her favorite chocolate bar in the middle (Joyce's favorite chocolate bar is a Midnight MilkyWay).

Please Note: There are seasons of life (e.g., sickness in the home, a new birth, moving to a new location, multiple children under 5 years of age, a job change, your mother-in-law moves in) when maintaining a home (washing dishes, cleaning the house, cutting the grass, buying groceries, managing bills, washing clothes, etc.) and maintaining sanity is enough, or possibly more than enough for any couple to accomplish. There are days when the best a couple can do is survive the demands placed upon them. Sometimes it is a wonderful day just to survive.

A FEW CLOSING REFLECTIONS
ON EXPECTATIONS

As noted earlier, your expectations of your wife and the degree to which she fulfills those expectations are a barometer for the level of marital satisfaction you feel in the marriage. If you are constantly frustrated with your wife due to some expectation, you need to evaluate what is taking place. The following steps have proved helpful to many husbands and should be beneficial to you.

Step One:
Ask yourself if the expectation you have of your wife is fair.

Why do you have this expectation? (Is your expectation based on your agreement with your wife, conversations with other husbands, an article you read in a magazine, roles performed by your parents when you were a child...etc.)

Note: If your expectation is based on something your Mama told you, as precious as she is, you may want to reconsider it.

Step Two:
Evaluate the manner you have communicated your expectation to your wife. (Have you effectively communicated your expectation to your wife?)

Too many couples fail to communicate their feelings about important issues to one another. If something is a concern, you have a responsibility to discuss your concern with your wife. I have worked with some couples who have allowed annoying issues to remain "unexpressed" for over 10 years.

Is it possible your wife has no clear understanding of your expectation? If this expectation is important to you, you need to clearly communicate how you feel about it to your wife.

What do you do if:

1. You are confident your expectation is fair.
2. You have clearly communicated your expectation to your wife. (Go to Step Three!)

Step Three:
In certain cases, a husband should take ownership of his expectation, stop holding his wife responsible for his frustration, and take action to solve the issue.

Here is a good example: Robert and Beth were a newlywed couple who had been married 6 months. Both Beth and Robert worked quite hard at their respective jobs. Overall, they described their marriage as "going ok." However, Beth had insisted they meet with me because of Robert's recent moodiness and irritability. As I talked with them, Robert shared how he felt things were going well in the marriage. Regarding the tension in the marriage, Robert mentioned he had recently received a promotion at work, and he thought Beth was probably picking up on the added stress he was experiencing from his job. However, when Beth stepped out of my office to go to the rest room, Robert looked at me and said, "Soap scum, the shower stall is always covered in soap scum!"

Bottom Line: In Robert's mind, he had assigned the cleaning of the glass shower stall to Beth because it was something his mother had done. As the soap scum built up on the shower door, so did his irritation with Beth. As is true with many couples, little irritations fester and bleed over into other interactions (...and little irritations can become major infections). Soap scum on a shower door is trivial to some, but for Robert it had evolved into a significant issue. He felt it was very important to have a clean shower area.

In this case, the resolution came by helping Robert accept his responsibilities in maintaining the home. Beth would have accepted the task, however, in situations like this it is usually best for the person with the concern (if possible) to take ownership of performing the task. In Robert and Beth's home, Robert has now assumed responsibility for cleaning the shower doors. He claimed ownership of his frustration.

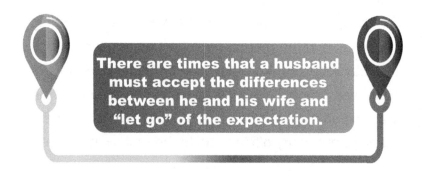

There are times that a husband must accept the differences between he and his wife and "let go" of the expectation.

Step Four:
There are times a husband must accept the differences between he and his wife and "let go" of the expectation. (Sometimes the best way to restore harmony in a marriage is for a husband to remove an expectation he has placed on his wife.)

Couples that I meet with, will typically tell me how the other spouse is messing up, letting them down, or doing them wrong. Any two people are going to have differences. If we are not careful, our differences can tear us apart. Sometimes we need to listen to each other, honestly share how we feel, and at the end of it, lovingly accept each other as we agree to disagree.

Think about it. You may be allowing an expectation you have of your wife to rob you of happiness. In some cases, the best thing to do is to adjust your expectations. One young husband told me that this revelation was a turning point for him in his marriage, enabling him to lay aside frustrations he had built up towards his wife. He was jolted by the reality that if he let go of an expectation he had of his wife; he could actually be happier in his marriage.

In reading the previous statements, you may think that compromise in this manner is not being fair to yourself (and granted, if the expectation is helping a couple have a healthy marriage it should not be negotiable). However, in some situations a husband will experience the greatest benefit by laying aside an expectation and gaining harmony in the marriage. It is also noteworthy, that for the Christian husband, sacrifice is one of the best paths to true fulfillment and satisfaction.

Chapter 3
Transform the Moment

We are all subject to the routines of doing what is necessary to maintain a home and to care for a family. It is not uncommon for today to seem like yesterday and for tomorrow to repeat the pattern. As we move through our days, it is a worthwhile endeavor to attempt to transform "moments" into a "memory" your wife can carry with her for weeks, months, or years to come.

These moments can serve as mental "keepsakes" which can build up and encourage your wife. These moments can be used by her, to help her feel cared for and loved. Don't allow yourself to be caught solely in the routine of the day. Don't allow yourself to become numb to the potential before you. Transform a moment!

As a warrior, as a man of God, moments and events in your home should be better because of your presence. Think about it: Here is this moment in time just waiting to be used by you to create something better, to transform it for good. Because of your words, your presence, your actions, a moment that would have been lifeless, or painful, or mundane is turned into this wonderful moment where something special happens. Maybe you make some gesture that helps your wife feel loved, or maybe you say something to lift her spirits.

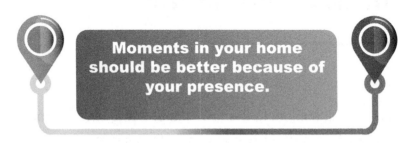

Moments in your home should be better because of your presence.

You and I both have limited moments. You have a limited number of words that you can say in your lifetime. You have a limited number of actions you can perform. You cannot afford to be careless with the moments that God gives you. Many moments can be transformed by a simple act or gesture. Moments can be transformed by the wink of an eye, a gentle smile, a kind word, a tender embrace.

It is a meaningful endeavor to "stay mindful" of the difference you can make in your wife's life. There are so many moments, each having the potential to bring her encouragement or pleasure. It is impossible to transform every moment, however, why not set a goal of transforming at least one moment each day by a simple action or word.

A CHALLENGE

In chapter 2 we used the term "neutral encounters" to refer to actions which are performed regularly to maintain home and family. Select a neutral encounter and develop a plan to transform the moment by creating a pleasing and special memory (maybe one that will last a lifetime).

An Example:

Christiana and Sal divided "home responsibilities" according to inside the house and outside the house. They often help each other in both domains but Sal carries the main responsibility for outside the home (it is several acres and very time consuming).

One week in early spring, Christiana was out of town for work. Sal took the opportunity to not only do the necessary work to maintain the yard, but in addition he spent several days planting her favorite flowers and creating beautiful hanging baskets which he hung on the front porch of the house. Sal created a beautiful entranceway lined with flowers leading to the front door of the house. When Christiana arrived home, the front area of the home was so beautiful it brought her to tears. Sal took a task that we could have labeled a "neutral encounter" for his marriage, and he transformed the moment creating a wonderful memory for Christiana that will possibly last a lifetime.

As a Man of God, Be A Transformer!

GUIDE TO A **GOOD MARRIAGE**

Chapter 4
Got Game?

There was a phrase originating several years ago, "Got Game," which was often used as a statement to indicate a person was good at some game or activity. If you had "Game," you had the skills and ability to excel at a certain task. As husbands, it would be awesome if we could reach the point in our marriage, where the people around us, our children and our friends, think of us as a husband whose "Got Game."

Do you know of men in your life who have "Game" when it comes to marriage? We need men who have that testimony. Maybe you can be that person for the friends in your life. I have friends who have "Game."

My dear friend Larry is a husband whose "Got Game." Larry and Martha Lynn have been married for 40 years. I hesitate to tell you one of the acts of "niceness" that Larry does for Martha Lynn because he makes most of us husbands look bad. Nonetheless, Larry's example may be something you want to do to "Be Nice" to your wife. When Martha Lynn takes a shower or a bath, Larry puts her bath towel in the dryer to warm it for her. When Martha Lynn's bath is over, Larry removes the towel from the dryer and presents it to her. (For all you men who are shaking your heads in disbelief, you may want to tear this page out of the book over fear that your wife may read it.)

Lamar is another dear friend of mine who is a wonderful husband. Lamar and Ann were married for 66 years (sadly Ann passed away recently). Many of you are probably painfully aware, but Covid 19 and the pandemic of 2020/2021 made it very difficult on families who had a family member in the hospital because of the restrictions on visitation. Unfortunately, Ann was in the hospital for 2 weeks and Lamar was not able to visit her.

During this time, Lamar was a great testimony to all husbands in the manner he would constantly encourage Ann and affirm her beauty. In fact, Lamar was always making a point of telling Ann she was pretty. If you spent the evening with Ann and Lamar, at some point you would hear Lamar tell Ann, "You sure are pretty."

Occasionally, Ann would make fun of Lamar's comments, making statements like, "You need to get your glasses," but Lamar never tired of reminding her.

When Ann was in the hospital, even though he could not be with her, he would continually call her. Listening to him one day as he spoke to Ann on the phone, it was quite inspiring to hear his tender and loving words to her. Lamar called her room at the hospital and talking to her on her phone said, "Even though I can't see you, I've been knowing you long enough to know that you are downright pretty." It is a wise and faithful husband who continues to remind his wife of her beauty.

How is your game when it comes to marriage? Are you even in the game? Are you working on perfecting your skills? I can remember how I practiced different sports when I was younger. For basketball, I would stand at the free throw line and take shot after shot so I could hopefully hit the foul shots in the game. I loved playing tennis, and hour upon hour I would practice my serve so when I played my opponents, I could hit the ball in the service square. Becoming good at a sport does not happen by accident.

When it comes to marriage, for others to be able to say of you, "He's Got Game," at least two things need to occur. First of all, you need to develop the skills of the game. Secondly, you need to get in the game.

DEVELOP THE SKILLS

I hope as you read through this book, you will gain information and insights that will assist you in developing your "marriage skills." As mentioned, a good marriage does not happen by accident. You cannot take your marriage for granted. If you do nothing, you cannot expect to have a good marriage. Expecting a good marriage while investing nothing would be like walking up to the starting line of a marathon race with no preparation or training and expecting to win the race. This would be a ludicrous endeavor and a recipe for a painful afternoon (if you even managed to make it across the finish line). To be able to place such strenuous demands on your body, you have to invest the work to train before you can achieve the desired results. If you are not investing anything into your marriage, what can you expect? I believe you are guaranteed a mediocre marriage and a wife who feels neglected.

Knee injuries have made it impossible for me to be a long-distance runner, but I have always enjoyed working out at a gym. One of the frustrating things about working out and developing strength is that strength actually diminishes if you don't stay consistently engaged. The skills in your marriage are no different and will diminish over time. You'd never get under the bar to bench press 200 LBs when you have not done it in years. Why do we do this with our marriage? Develop your marriage skills and keep practicing.

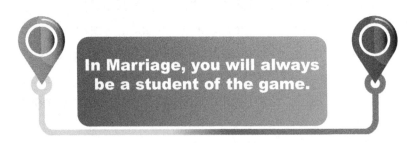

In Marriage, you will always be a student of the game.

When it comes to marriage, you will always need to be a Student of the Game, and an Active Participant. Truly, in marriage we are all Lifetime Learners!

GET IN THE GAME!

For a football player, it would be very frustrating to be "dressed out" to play a game, but never get in the game. At the end of a game, there is honor in being among those whose jerseys are soiled with blood, sweat, and grass stains. In some ways, there is embarrassment for the player who walks off the field with a clean jersey. It proclaims to all who sees the player, that he never "got in the game."

Please don't just read through this book. Be intentional and get in the game. My prayer is that one day you will be the husband that others point to and exclaim, "He's really Got Game!"

GUIDE TO A **GOOD MARRIAGE**

Chapter 5
Clothe Yourself

Several years ago, I was asked to speak at the baccalaureate service of a local high school. In preparing the message, I contacted the mother of one of the graduating seniors (a very tall young man) and asked for some of his baby clothes. As he stood before hundreds of people in his cap and gown, I held up a very small outfit he wore when he was two years old. The point to be made was that there was a day when this little outfit was appropriate clothing for him. Not only that, in his infant years his mom and dad clothed him. He did not pick out his clothes and he did not put them on his body. However, today was a day he selected his clothing and dressed himself. Today with a cap and gown, this young man was dressed in a manner that clearly portrayed his involvement in a graduation service.

How you clothe yourself speaks to the intent of your day.

Most of you who are reading this book are not naked. If you are naked, I am sure you have a good reason. Nonetheless, like our young graduate, when you were a small child your mom or dad chose the clothes you wore and dressed you. As you grew older, you began to choose your clothing and to assume responsibility for dressing yourself. This morning, you selected the items of clothing you put on. From the many items in your closet, you made a choice as to what you felt would be most appropriate for your day.

When it comes to marriage, you have a choice as to the "clothes" you wear. When you are at work, there may be specific expectations of the clothes you must wear. When you are watching a sports event, you possibly dress yourself to identify with "Your Team." When you are with your wife, you need to make the choice to clothe yourself with kindness. You need to **"Be Nice."** Be intentional with this decision.

Scripture clearly proclaims the clothes we should wear. Colossians 3: 12 states, "Therefore, as God's chosen people, holy and dearly loved, clothe yourselves with compassion, kindness, humility, gentleness and patience."

Allow me to echo the importance of this verse: When you are with your wife, you choose the manner you clothe yourself. Don't bring your dirty clothes home from work or other places. Don't "cop out" acting like someone else clothed you today. Don't act surprised by what you are wearing. Don't blame someone else for the manner you are clothed. The clothes are on you . . . Own It! Purposefully and intentionally, clothe yourself with kindness. **"Be Nice!"**

BUT THERE ARE TIMES WHEN I DON'T FEEL NICE

True, in life there are times we do not feel nice. Without question, some days are extremely tough (the children prevented you from sleeping, a crazed maniac cut in front of you on the highway, the waitress was soooo slow in bringing you your food at the restaurant and you are fairly sure it was on purpose). However, feelings do not necessarily determine who we are. Feelings do not necessarily determine what we do. Everyone has a bad day. Everyone has moments when they feel irritable or exhausted. Our goal, in the midst of horrible, terrible, very bad days….is still to "Be Nice."

It is important for us to recognize that as husbands we are fully capable of expressing love and kindness, even in those moments when we don't feel loving. You can be nice, even though you don't feel nice. You can express love even when you don't feel loving.

Your wife doesn't deserve less just because the world gave you less today. If you are waiting on the perfect day to be nice to your wife, you will be waiting a long time and your marriage will suffer while you wait on the world to be nice to you.

ACTING YOUR WAY TO A FEELING

One day Phil met with me to announce he no longer loved his wife. (As noted with Ryan and Erica, this is a statement I have heard from numerous couples.) After talking with Phil about his recent interactions with his wife Hannah, I asked him, "When you loved Hannah, what things did you do to express that love to her?" Phil responded by giving examples such as:

- Leave her notes around the house
- Give her flowers
- Call her during the day "Just to say Hi"

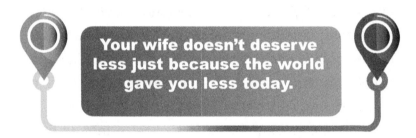

Your wife doesn't deserve less just because the world gave you less today.

After his comments, I asked Phil if he would start doing some of those "expressions of love." As you might expect, Phil replied by saying, "But I don't have the same feelings. I don't love her." Even though he did not have the "feelings" I asked him to act upon what was right for a Christian husband to do to express love to his wife.

Ultimately, Phil agreed to demonstrate "expressions of love" to Hannah for the next several months.

Four months later Phil came to me to admit that his feelings had begun to change. It was as if his love was reawakened. Time and again, I have seen wonderful changes occur when a husband does not use his "feelings" as an excuse to alter the way he acts toward his wife. Without question, you can act your way into a feeling, especially when that action is one that honors God, as in the case when a husband chooses to express love to his wife.

As a Christian husband, a man of God who is seeking to honor our Lord, there are important questions that you must ask yourself when you believe your feelings for your wife have faded.

1. **What is more important, to be faithful to God or to be faithful to a feeling?**
2. **Is it more important to be the husband God would have me to be, or to use my feelings as an excuse to act irresponsibly to my wife?**

Countless husbands have used their "feelings" as a justification to be faithless in their marriage relationship. Don't make that mistake. As a Christian husband, take charge of your feelings.

WHEN "BEING NICE" IS BEYOND OUR ABILITY

When I was young, I watched a movie about aliens who planted seeds in humans in order to propagate the alien race. For a young boy, it was scary enough that it left some mental images I can still recall. Has an alien life-form planted seeds in you which are giving birth to a crazed, sadistic, person whose goal is to be hostile towards his wife with antagonistic and hurtful words?

Even though unlikely, let's say you believe an alien has planted "seeds" in you which cause you to periodically lose control and behave cruelly towards your wife. What should you do on days when you are not the best version of you?

When you are Husband Negative 2.0 Instead of version 10.0, What should you do?

If you can't Be Nice, if there are days when it is beyond your skill set to be kind, you should communicate this clearly to your wife. Isn't that fair? Don't you want your wife informing you of days when she has one nerve left, and you are in the vicinity to step on it? Don't you want to know when she is on the edge of pulling out her hair in disgust? If there is a day when she is not fit to be around man nor beast, wouldn't you want to know? Similarly, if you are a walking landmine ready to explode at any moment, shouldn't you convey that fact to your wife? It might help prevent an explosion that could take somebody's life. And as it has been said, *"The life you save may be your own!"*

Chapter 6
A Time to Matter

Josh is great guy….and I know his question, "Will I ever matter?" was heart felt. But I had to tell him, "No."

Now this simple reply was not a statement regarding his self-worth. I was not implying that I thought Josh did not matter. Josh is of ultimate value to God. Jesus gave his life for Josh. Jesus helps us all know how wonderfully valuable we are to Him. So yes, Josh matters, but when he asked me the question the most appropriate answer was "No." (Granted, I was hesitant to say "No" but Josh was asking the question in regard to his marriage.)

Prior to Josh asking this question, I had listened to him demean his wife with some unkind and harsh statements such as: his wife is a poor mother, she is mindless, and living with her was like living in hell.

(I don't think Josh had ever actually lived in Hell; however, I am sure he had heard from some preacher it was a very unpleasant place to live.)

For over an hour, I had listened to Josh try to establish the fact that he mattered more than his wife. So, to the question, "Will I ever matter?" for Josh the best answer is "No." If Josh wants to make sure he matters, his disagreements with his wife will always end up with puts downs and innuendos as he seeks to position himself as a person who matters more than his wife. **Josh's focus CANNOT BE on being a person who matters. Josh's focus has to be on ensuring that his wife matters.**

You might think it interesting, but Josh did not reject my response to him. He may have been somewhat disappointed at my reply, but he accepted what I said. I continued by explaining to Josh what I believe is true for me as well as every Christian husband. As a husband, my focus must be on expressing love for my wife.

As mentioned earlier, a good goal for you today is to leave your wife "better off" after your encounter with her. Reflect on the following question once again. How is your wife after an encounter with you?

If your wife's opinion of herself was based on your words and actions toward her, what would she believe about herself? If you were the only mirror in her life, would she know her beauty? As a husband, one of my primary goals is for Joyce to feel loved and valued.

She is a priceless treasure and a person of great beauty. As mentioned, I want to help her see herself as God sees her. For a husband, demeaning or hurtful statements to his wife are completely contrary to God's calling on his life.

It is a wonderful undertaking for a husband to affirm his wife's value, to help her know how much she matters. It is also the best path to gaining the satisfying relationship with your wife that you desire. Truly, the more your wife believes she matters to you, the more you will matter to her.

Our focus should not be self-indulgent. God's Word helps us understand that our focus is never on ourselves, on some self-inflating thought that "I Am Special." All of us have been around individuals who spend a lot of time telling us how much they matter. Seeking the spotlight, their conversations revolve around themselves. However, if you are always focused on yourself, you will neglect others. If you are always craving a mirror in a vain attempt to see

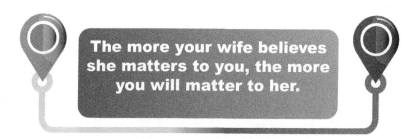

The more your wife believes she matters to you, the more you will matter to her.

your own reflection, it may be difficult to see others. In fact, you will probably look past (overlook) others in an attempt to see your own reflection.

Let me be clear (or redundant, but it is a very important point). You do matter. You are of ultimate value and unmeasurable worth. However, a problem occurs when your focus is on "mattering" or being noticed. Consequently, when a husband is focused on "mattering," he often loses focus of one of his primary objectives--making sure his wife matters.

Jesus is our example. As noted in a verse mentioned earlier, Ephesians 5:25 states, "Husbands, love your wives as Christ loved the church and gave Himself up for her."

How did Jesus love the church? How does He love you and me? Philippians 2:5-8 is a passage that helps us understand how Jesus' love was/is expressed. In these verses in Philippians, God's Word tells us we should seek to have the same mind as Jesus who gave up His rights and sacrificed His life for others. Jesus mattered, and His sacrifice helps us realize how much we matter to God.

A husband is "really wrong" when "being right" is more important to him than his wife.

Philippians 2:5. In your relationships with one another, have the same mindset as Christ Jesus: 6. Who, being in very nature of God, did not consider equality with God something to be used to His own advantage; 7. rather, He made Himself nothing by taking the very nature of a servant, being made in human likeness. 8. And being found in appearance as a man, He humbled Himself by becoming obedient to death—even death on a cross!

The "heart" of the husband should be focused on caring for his wife.

The "heart" of the husband should be focused on caring for his wife. I often tell a husband that I understand his wanting to be right. We typically always think we are right. Why would you have an opinion and believe it to be wrong? Proverbs 21:2 echoes this, "Every way of a man is right in his own eyes, but the Lord weighs the heart." Nonetheless, even though a husband is confident he is right, the times when he is actually wrong, is when being right is more important to him than his wife. Clearly, that is when you are really wrong. Being "right" should never be more important to you than your wife.

Truly, there are times you are better off "being wrong."

Too often our focus is on making sure our wife knows that we "have rights" (like a husband proclaiming, "I've Got My Rights"). Too often, our focus is on positioning ourselves through argument or conversational dialogue, to prove we "are right." When our focus is on being right, our energy is "spent" in the wrong endeavor. When the husband is leading out, seeking to always "be right," the wife will often follow his lead and expend her energy in the endeavor of "being right" as well. When husband and wife are expending all of their energy on "mattering" and on "being right" it is possible to end up with a marriage where neither husband nor wife feels that they matter. Sadly, sometimes the "one thing" husband and wife are sure of, is that they don't matter to each other.

As a husband, here is a wonderful goal for you. Let your focus be on helping your wife understand that she "Matters." As a husband focus your energy on helping your wife "Be Right!"

VALUE YOUR WIFE VALUE THE MARRIAGE

A young couple (Tony and Carol) came into my office. They were quite distraught with one another. In reality, I think Tony was mostly annoyed and Carol may have just been frustrated. The problem that brought them into my office was a dispute that began after Tony discovered Carol had spent 63 dollars on a pair of shoes.

After listening to Tony proclaim Carol's failings and financial indiscretions from the past, I asked Tony, "How much is your marriage worth to you?"

Tony made the wise response, stating he could not put a dollar value on his marriage. I simply said, "Yes you can, it is 63 dollars."

Years ago, there were balance scales that merely had two plates opposite each other. In some ways, the scale was similar to a seesaw on a children's playground. If the biggest kid in your class was seated opposite you on the seesaw, you might be catapulted off into the parking lot. Just like a seesaw, on this scale you could place an object on the plate on one side of the scale and on the other plate on the scale you could put weights enabling you to calculate the weight of the object.

If we could put your marriage on the plate on one side of the scale, what could we place on the plate on the other side of the scale that would carry more "weight," ... that would be more important to you than your marriage? What in your life is more valuable than your marriage? Is there a car, a computer or a tool, that is worth more than your marriage?

No doubt, there are certain objects that are quite important to you. This is true for all of us. However, husbands always lose when "stuff" is more valued than the marriage.

A Time to Matter

We need to always remember the tremendous value that God places on what He has joined together (Matthew 19:6). You need to value what God values. Your marriage is of supreme value. A great goal for all husbands is to continually remind themselves of the priority of their marriage.

ASSIGNMENT

1. In a future interaction with your wife, seek to help her Be Right… even at the cost of you being wrong.
2. Reflect on the following questions: Is there anything your wife may believe is more valuable to you than your marriage to her? If your marriage is truly a relationship of ultimate value to you, are there any changes that need to occur in your life?

Chapter 7
The Gift of "A Redo"

One of the most effective tools in redeeming moments in a marriage is when either husband or wife is willing to forgive the other person. Our goal is to redeem as many moments as possible. We want to live with a redemptive spirit.

In my initial meeting with a couple, I will often ask the couple if there is anything that is hindering the husband or wife from forgiving one another. Lack of forgiveness can create a significant barrier preventing a couple from maturing together as they should. Lack of forgiveness can rob a married couple of its joy as it anchors them to negative moments from the past.

You cannot live in the past and have a good marriage. Can you imagine a man attempting to drive his car forward while continually gazing at his rearview mirror? How could you possibly arrive at a good destination when you are always preoccupied with what is behind you? You need to be aware of the critical importance, and the value of "A Redo."

A GOOD MARRIAGE
REQUIRES FORGIVENESS

Forgiveness is a powerful gift and a needed expression in any marriage relationship. Holding on to something your wife has done or said that has hurt you instead of forgiving her, is a costly endeavor. Forgiveness is not just meaningful to your wife (as she becomes aware of the fact that you are not holding her missteps against her) but it is freeing to your own life.

When we refuse to forgive our wives, we are like a person carrying a backpack full of rocks. Every time we hold on to some action our wife has done wrong, we add one more rock to the backpack. We may attempt to convince ourselves that our bag of rocks is empowering. We may tell ourselves the rocks will be helpful, so we can have them available to throw at our wives in moments of conflict. However, the truth is, our bag of rocks will weigh us down.

Lack of forgiveness can rob a married couple of its joy as it anchors the couple to negative moments from the past.

If we continue in unforgiveness, the rocks we collect will eventually make any journey extremely burdensome. Ironically, it is common to believe that the grudges (rocks) we are holding on to are hurting our wives and helping us. Meanwhile, we are the ones with a sore back as we drag around our bag of rocks.

It is important to note that not all husbands throw rocks at their wives. Some are too quiet or reserved to raise their voice and sling the rock. However, they do something that can actually be more dangerous. . . they use the rocks to build. They collect each small rock and mortar them together to build a boulder. Eventually this boulder will become so massive and large that it is virtually immovable. Without forgiveness, it is now a fixture on their mental landscape. Every time this husband attempts to look at his wife, there is now this horrific obstruction that hinders his view.

FREED THROUGH FORGIVENESS

One of the wonderful things about forgiveness is that it prevents a day from being stolen from us because of one lapse of judgment in our actions or one careless comment.

For example: Joyce and I were taking a group from our church to a marriage enrichment conference in North Carolina. We had two vans to transport our seven couples. For the first half of the trip, we rode in the vans as couples, but after a wonderful lunch at the Dillard House (a popular destination restaurant in Georgia) we

The Gift of "A Redo" 59

strategically divided up in a way we thought would be most enriching. The guys were in the first van (so we could talk about "guy stuff") and the girls followed in the second van. I was driving the first van, and Joyce was driving the second van (her request).

About ten minutes after leaving the Dillard House, the second van started flashing its headlights (except for emergencies, no cell phone use was allowed) and honking its horn in an attempt to get the first van to pull over into a junk yard (the ladies later corrected me saying it was a Craft Fair...but it looked like a junk yard). Unfortunately, my foot slipped, and we went speeding past the "Craft Fair."

Actually, my foot did not slip, but stopping so soon after a lunch break was unacceptable, and the loss of time would have been costly. I had one goal on my mind. I wanted to arrive as soon as possible at the marriage conference, and another delay would potentially put us in heavy traffic in the Ashville area.

When we arrived at the marriage conference, the girls were not happy. In fact, I was stunned Joyce was so upset. Joyce stepped out of the van and looked at me and said, "That's One!" Fortunately, after a few minutes she seemed to be back to her sweet self. Guess what saved me? Before we left the church, we had agreed that we would extend three acts of forgiveness (we called them Redo's) to each other on our marriage enrichment weekend.

In the best of marriages, there will be actions committed or words spoken that are not received well by the husband or wife. I believe a "Redo" is effective because at the heart of most couples is the desire to "get along" and be at peace. However, our differences quite often put us at odds with one another. We will always have differing opinions on various issues in life. One of us will always miscommunicate, misstep, make an error due to impatience, or do a host of other things which have the ability to annoy or irritate our spouse.

There are times when the main function of a "Redo" is to simply forgive your spouse that she does not think like you or interpret life like you. When I drove past the "Craft Fair," I was not attempting to disregard Joyce's "wants" or intentionally trying to annoy her. I thought I was acting in the best interest of the group. Nonetheless, in my actions I angered her. If she had not issued me a "Redo" I can guarantee our first night at the conference would not have been very enjoyable for us, and the anger or resentment from day 1 could have easily carried over to the next day and impacted the entire weekend.

Couples I have counseled have told me that this one act, a willingness to give at least one "forgiveness" or "Redo" a day, has significantly changed the level of conflict in their home. As one husband said, "Our home has not been like this in years, ...maybe ever." The agreement he had made with his wife (a few months prior to his statement) was that he and his wife would give each other one "Redo" a day.

I have told young couples leaving on vacations, to give each other five acts of forgiveness to ensure

The Gift of "A Redo" 61

a special vacation trip does not turn into a nightmare. This may sound trivial, or unrealistic, but from years of experience I have found the gift of the "Redo" to be a powerful tool in the life of a Christian couple to help maintain harmony (peace) in the home. When practiced, it is a simple, but extremely effective tool in maintaining a good marriage. It will help you keep joy in your day. It helps prevent a sunny day from becoming a day of rain and dark clouds. I also believe it is in fulfillment of what Jesus would have us to do.

It is an extremely wise husband who during the course of a day forgives his wife. At the end of the day, this is the husband who is able to count the blessings of his marriage instead of the faults of his wife. If not already, I hope you will mature into a husband who chooses to be "Quick to Forgive."

REFLECTIONS

Reflect on the manner forgiveness is extended by you to your wife. Are you quick to forgive your wife or are her missteps "held in storage" to be used against her in moments when you are attempting to win an argument? Is there something for which you need to forgive your wife?

ASSIGNMENT

Search heart and mind for "unforgiveness" that you are harboring against your wife. If there is nothing, Great! If you find a "bag of rocks," write the items out in list form.

Looking at the items, one by one, pray for the strength to free yourself from the bondage of unforgiveness in your life. Pray for the strength to forgive and to "Let It Go!"

Exercise: Take a deep breath. As you breathe out, think of it as releasing the toxic "unforgiveness" you have been harboring in your body, soul and mind. Breathe in again, as you breathe in, think of it as "breathing in" God's Life-Giving Forgiveness--a gift that you are prepared to share with your wife when needed.

**Breathe Out and Breathe In Regularly.
It is Nurturing for Mind, Body, and Soul.**

WHEN YOU CAN'T FORGIVE

When the severity of pain from an event is substantial the ability to forgive may be difficult or delayed. In certain situations, extended time is required for forgiveness. Forgiveness becomes a process.

Forgiveness may need to be proclaimed time and again before true forgiveness is experienced. For example, you wake up on Monday and proclaim to

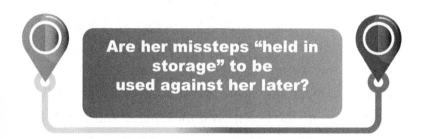

Are her missteps "held in storage" to be used against her later?

yourself your desire to extend forgiveness in a certain matter, and you pray for God's help in this endeavor. However, on Monday evening your heart still aches, and you experience seeds of bitterness and resentment still trying to take root in your life. You wake up Tuesday morning and proclaim your desire to extend forgiveness (regarding the same issue) and you pray for God's help. On Tuesday evening you sense feelings of indignation and pains of betrayal which seem to cycle over and over in your mind. You wake up Wednesday morning proclaiming your desire to extend forgiveness and you pray for God's help.

Much like the movie *Groundhog Day*, you keep letting go of that "rock" but it ends up back in your back pack the next day. It is as if the same day is replayed over and over. This pattern may repeat for weeks. Even when you feel you have truly been set free from the bondage of an event; something may happen that seemingly throws you back to an unhealthy place where you once again are wanting to lash out at the person you believe has wronged you. However, in time you will accomplish your goal of forgiveness.

The previous paragraphs on forgiveness are not presented to frustrate you or to make you feel as if forgiveness is impossible. Be assured, bondage to an event is never so strong or intense that you cannot free yourself and extend forgiveness. However, it is important to recognize that there are situations where forgiveness takes a significant amount of time and effort. No doubt, as a Christian husband you may have the desire

to forgive hours, days, or weeks before the actual forgiveness occurs. Forgiveness is sometimes born out of
days of struggle. Persevere and forgiveness will come.

THE BONDAGE OF UNFORGIVENESS

You can probably think of a friend who is always sharing
the various ways his wife has wronged him or actions
she has committed to irritate him. I have emails from
counselees complaining about perceived wrongdoings
their spouses committed more than 20 years ago. Don't
be that guy. You need to set your wife free; you need to
set yourself free.

One afternoon a young lady came to my office
to receive a "divorce blessing." Earlier that day she had
met with a lawyer to begin the legal process of divorc-
ing her husband. Basically, she wanted me to tell her
that she was justified in her actions.

Three years prior, she had an affair with a
co-worker. Remorseful, she confessed the affair to her
husband and asked for his forgiveness. After several
weeks of emotional highs and lows, her husband told
her he did not want to end the marriage. He told his wife
he forgave her and wanted to start afresh. No doubt,
he had good intentions and his desire was admirable
(many men are not willing to continue in the marriage
after an affair). Unfortunately, his forgiveness was con-
ditional. It was not "true" forgiveness.

The reason this young lady filed for divorce was
because she felt as if she was continually living in the

shadow of her affair. Every time she and her husband had an argument, she said he would use her affair against her. For three years, it had become his trump card he would pull out to win important arguments as he would proclaim, "Well, you are the one who had the affair!" She felt she could no longer live under such oppression.

Please note: As is so often true, here were two wonderful people. Unfortunately, instead of finding happiness they were living in the "land of oz." The wife, a precious Christian, was trying to deal with her own shame regarding the affair. However, it was not a wizard behind a curtain she needed. She was wanting to be assured of God's forgiveness. She yearned for a fresh start. As the husband was working through his own grief about the affair, he failed to see the importance of his role in helping his wife know God's forgiveness and grace. Each time he reminded her of the affair, she felt as if she was anchored to her sin in such a way that she would never be free. Finally, she began to believe her only chance to be free of the affair was to be free of her husband.

I did not "bless" her divorce. I told her, "Before you try divorce, I wish you would try marriage." Fortunately, with her husband actively seeking her forgiveness and coming to a better understanding of what forgiveness on his part should look like, she was willing to continue with counseling, and begin her own process of forgiving him. Six years later, the couple is still doing quite well.

The Gift of Forgiveness

It is important to remember that forgiveness is not deserved or earned. Forgiveness is a gift to give and receive. Your wife should not have to suffer for years to experience this forgiveness from you, it is a gift... no strings attached.

I am sure you are thankful for God's forgiveness in your life. God's forgiveness is a cleansing forgiveness. We are forgiven and justified through Jesus Christ. As the old preacher would say, "Through Jesus you are Justified, it is 'Just as If' you had never sinned." First John 1:9 proclaims this wonderful truth, "If we confess our sins, He is faithful and just to forgive us our sins and to cleanse us from all unrighteousness."

As you receive God's forgiveness, try your best to mirror God's forgiveness in your daily interactions with your wife. In fact, God's Word warns us that if we refuse to forgive, it interferes with us being able to receive God's forgiveness. Matthew 6:14 states, "For if you forgive other people when they sin against you, your heavenly Father will also forgive you. 15. But if

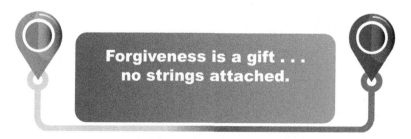

Forgiveness is a gift . . .
no strings attached.

you do not forgive others their sins, your Father will not forgive your sins."

ASSIGNMENT

As you find security and peace through God's forgiveness, pray that you can continue to grow in your ability to extend forgiveness and grace to your wife. Give your wife the gift of at least "One Redo" a day. Sometimes you will say nothing and merely grant the gift. On other occasions, you may need to tell your wife of some action she committed that hurt or annoyed you. (You may be thinking, I don't want to say anything to her that might "rock the boat." However, it is better to rock the boat than allow irritations to fester that might one day "sink the ship." Openness and honesty in a marriage is always a priority.)

Colossians 3:13. Bear with each other and forgive one another if any of you has a grievance against someone. Forgive as the Lord forgave you. 14. And over all these virtues put on love, which binds them all together in perfect unity.

Chapter 8
The Good, the Bad & the Smelly

The title of this chapter may sound absurd but please take it seriously. I will be brief and to the point. **The bottom line: You need to smell good to your wife.**

Through the years, on numerous occasions, I have listened to young wives express their concern for the way their husbands smell. Comments from wives about bad breath, feet or shoe odor, underarm odor, or general body odor have been made to me about "smelly husbands."

One fact you may not know (information that is quite important), is that a woman has a better sense of smell than a man. I was totally unaware of this until my sweet-smelling wife Joyce, my anatomy and physiology expert, told me. As astounding as it sounds, it is true. Your wife can smell odors that you cannot smell. It is probably one of the reasons a Bath and Body Works is full of women and not men. Joyce addresses this topic in our upcoming book, A *Guide to a Good Marriage: Sex and the Christian Couple.* Hence, it is not fair for me to say too much about it. Nevertheless, knowledge of a woman's outstanding ability to smell odors, illuminates the importance of a husband asking his wife to let him know if he needs to perform any action (brush teeth, bathe, sand blast feet) to enhance his "aroma."

Some husbands may find it easy to make light of this topic (granted it could be somewhat comical), however, we really need to be sensitive to our wives. Certain wives, especially those recently married, have a difficult time making statements that are critical of their husbands. The fact is, you may be killing your wife with your breath or other body odors, yet in her concern over the possibility of upsetting you, she is continuing to breathe your toxic smell and not say anything.

All of us have been around someone who has bad breath or an unpleasant body odor. This is not typically a person you want to be close to for very long. What if that person is you? Would it bother you to know that you are the guy at work who everyone dreads to be "in their face." Wouldn't you want to know? Wouldn't you want to do something about it?

You may find this surprising, but I have met with young couples where the wife has expressed difficulty in being intimate with her husband because of his "breath." Do you want your wife growing in her distaste of you, or concerned about being sexually intimate with you because you smell bad? The fact is, breath and body odor can be a significant sexual deterrent for any marriage.

This is clearly not a time to, "Pull a Jack." Remember, Jack from chapter 2. He is the guy that basically, said, "This is me, this is who I am. Accept me as I am, if you don't like it, too bad." If a husband has feet that stink, his wife needs to tell him. If a husband's breath is bad, a wife should feel the freedom to let him know right away. In no way should a husband be sensitive or defensive about a wife telling him he "stinks." Maybe God gave wives the better sense of smell to help husbands be at their best.

ASSIGNMENT

Tell your wife you have learned that she has a better sense of smell than you. Explain to her that you want to be your best for her and that you need her to tell you when she thinks you need to do better in bathing, dental hygiene.... etc. Reiterate the fact that she is helping you when she tells you, and you would deeply appreciate her honesty. (Don't be surprised if she replies, "I have wanted to say something, I didn't want to hurt your feelings, but your ....")

Before we leave this topic, I have asked Joyce to share with you a few facts behind the statement, "A woman smells better than a man," no pun intended.

The Good, the Bad & the Smelly

Dan: Joyce, is it true that a woman can smell odors that a man cannot?

Joyce: Yes, this is definitely true, and it has been verified through scientific research.

Dan: Can you help us guys understand how this is possible?

Joyce: To put it simply, women are better equipped to smell differing odors. In clinical studies, using a method called isotropic fractionator, researchers discovered that women have 40% more cells than men in the olfactory bulb in the brain. Olfactory cells are the ones that allow us to identify differing odors. For those tested, this increased sensitivity was five orders of magnitude greater for women than for men. Certain odors were not even detected by the guys, even with practice.

Dan: So, men are inferior to women?

Joyce: A point that could be made, but it is better to just say men and women are different. However, when it comes to an ability to smell, it is critical to understand that while a man is not sensing any odor

GUIDE TO A **GOOD MARRIAGE**

at all, it is possible that a woman is being overwhelmed by an unpleasant odor.

Dan: Why would God equip a woman differently than a man?

Joyce: It is impossible to know all of God's ways. Men are such great protectors of the family. Maybe God tuned a man's ability to smell in such a way that a man would not be repulsed by a smell that would make a woman run and hide. Men are a quite courageous in facing the most difficult of situations.

Dan: Given our differences, do you have any advice for husbands?

Joyce: I do think it is important for husbands to acknowledge a woman's ability to smell odors that he cannot. He needs to respect what she says about a certain odor. Plus, please remember, if you are smelling some odor, there is the possibility that the intensity of that smell is five times greater for your wife.

I think it would be easy for any husband to disregard his wife's statements about

The Good, the Bad & the Smelly

"what she smells." However, this would be frustrating for any woman. It is quite unfortunate, but a woman's heightened ability to smell odors could result in some difficult situations for a married couple.

Dan: For example, selecting a hotel room for a couple's "weekend getaway."

Joyce: Danny knows how true this is for me. When we enter a hotel room, it is important to me that there is a fresh pleasant scent in the room. There have been times when I would smell a certain odor and think to myself, "This is not a room where I feel comfortable." An unpleasant odor makes it impossible for me to enjoy staying in a room.

After we enter a hotel room, Danny, who is often jumping on the bed, typically does not smell anything. Yet, in his respect for me, he will always ask for another room. If Danny were to downplay my concern over the odor, or to deny that the odor exists, because he cannot smell it, it would be hurtful to me, and damaging to our evening together.

Dan: What about the way I smell?

Joyce: A funny question, I think you smell springtime fresh. But yes, to the point of your question, it is important that a husband take seriously his own self-care when it comes to odors. As you have mentioned, it is an astute husband who enlists his wife to help him maintain a high standard of self-care. I think it is a wise husband who extends to his wife the right to let him know when he needs to put on more deodorant or take a breath mint.

Dan: You are also addressing this topic in more detail in our book, *A Guide to a Good Marriage: Sex and the Christian Couple.*

Joyce: Right, this is quite an intriguing topic. It is also interesting to recognize how differing scents can impact us. An amazing God made a complex and amazing man and woman.

Chapter 9
A Sexual Adventure

Through the years, I have met with numerous couples who are struggling in their sexual relationship. Some couples ask to meet with me acknowledging their need to find help with sexual issues. Other couples, hesitant to mention the word "sex," come stating they are in conflict, only to discover the real issue resides in the bitterness and resentment that was birthed from their dismal sexual relationship.

Presently, Joyce and I are working on a book entitled, *A Guide to a Good Marriage: Sex and the Christian Couple*, which is entirely devoted to a couple's sexual relationship. This chapter is somewhat of a primer for what you will find in that book. Let's begin by mentioning some important truths for husbands.

1. Sex is good for a marriage.

2. In the majority of marriages (but not all), the husband has the stronger sexual drive.

3. Sex is sometimes the root of deep frustrations for a husband.

4. In the majority of marriages, the husband is the initiator of the sexual events that occur in the marriage.

5. In the majority of marriages, there is extremely poor communication regarding "sex in marriage" (unless you consider the statement, "You wanna do it tonight?" communication).

6. A husband who relegates his sexual relationship with his wife to serendipitous encounters (happenchance) will often find their sexual relationship a continual source of conflict.

SEXUALLY STARVING

I hope the sexual relationship in your marriage is going well. However, if you are encountering difficulty in that area, you are not alone. Joyce and I have taught conferences and workshops on the topic of "sex," for thousands of couples. In many of those workshops we presented husbands and wives with a sheet containing a list of statements that expressed various feelings, attitudes, or opinions on sex (the list was created from comments made by husbands and wives during counseling). After distributing the list to each attendee, husbands and wives were asked to select the top three statements (in graded order) which best reflected their current feelings or attitudes. It is noteworthy that the number 1 answer, for 1 out of every 6.5 husbands was, "I am sexually starving." (This was an informal survey, which over the past 20 years, has been handed out to over 3000 married men at marriage conferences.) Granted, the informal manner in which the survey was handed out and collected prevents us from making specific claims pertaining to the general marriage population (ie: claiming 1 out of every 6.5 husbands is sexually starving). However, the response of over a thousand husbands does give us reason to claim that many men are dissatisfied with the regularity of "sex" in their marriage.

Please note: In making the statement, "1 out of every 6.5 husbands are sexually starving," it is important to acknowledge that there are wives who are frustrated because of their husbands' disinterest in sex. For many years I have listened to both husbands and wives share their frustrations regarding what is, or what is not occurring in their sexual relationships. Numerous women have shared their concerns over their husbands' disinterest in sex. Furthermore, in surveys with married couples that Joyce and I have distributed, approximately 20 percent of the wives claim to have the dominant sexual thirst. Without question, some wives are exasperated when they hear that it is the husband who is always the sexual aggressor.

Truly, for many husbands and wives, their sexual relationship is a point of deep frustration.

A Sexual Adventure   79

BUT WHAT IS A GUY TO DO WHEN HIS DREAM OF MARITAL SEXUAL BLISS IS MORE OF A BLIZZARD?

Carolyn called and asked if she and Cedric could meet me at my house that evening. Carolyn said, "Cedric asked me to let him tell you about our situation."

Upon meeting with them, and before Carolyn had fully sat in a chair, Carolyn blurted out, "He is being unfaithful." After which Cedric was quick to respond that he would never be unfaithful.

Cedric said, "Look, I don't know what to do. Every time I hint at wanting sex, she is quick to tell me it is not a good time. The truth is, there is never a good time with her. Watching movies with good 'love scenes' is kind of satisfying to me."

With this Carolyn exclaimed, "Watching was not all he was doing when I walked in."

Cedric glared at Carolyn and angrily replied, "Carolyn, what do you expect. That's right, I was masturbating. The scene in the movie was exciting and I masturbated to it."

Carolyn replied, "It makes me feel as if I am not enough."

Growing more agitated Cedric exclaimed to Carolyn, "Are you kidding me. How can you even say that? Almost every day I ask if we can be together. You always say no. You never want to be with me. At least this way I don't have to deal with your rejection!"

CEDRIC AND CAROLYN

It may not sound like it, but Cedric and Carolyn are a couple that most members in the church would consider the ideal couple with the ideal family. Personally, I think they are both quite awesome. Both Cedric and Carolyn are very active in church. They are both faithful and committed Christians with wonderful hearts. They are the kind of people that would do almost anything to help a person in need. Anyone would be fortunate to call either Cedric or Carolyn a friend. Unfortunately, the stressors of life have started to cause serious tension in their marriage. Like many couples, Cedric and Carolyn are at a point where they need to readjust some priorities and focus on taking care of one another.

AN OVERWHELMED LIFE

Both Cedric and Carolyn are living a life that is very full. Both work full time jobs. They are both involved in various leadership (servanthood) roles at church. Not only are their children involved in our sports program at church but both Cedric and Carolyn help coach their teams. During the soccer season, combining normal church activities and sports activities, they find themselves away from home most evenings.

The words that Carolyn and Cedric used to describe their lives were: busy, overcommitted, overwhelmed, and tired. (Typically, a guy can feel this way and look at his wife and proclaim, "Let's have sex." Typically, a wife feeling this way proclaims, "Let's go to bed... and go to sleep.") Cedric and Carolyn were doing a lot of wonderful activities. Unfortunately, in the midst of a very active life they were beginning to lose sight of one another. Cedric and Carolyn were doing a lot of wonderful activities, but they were not doing what was best for their marriage or their children.

THE SOLUTION

You might find it reassuring to know that Cedric and Carolyn were able to dramatically improve their relationship within a few weeks. The solution that was instrumental in helping them has been helpful to numerous couples. Simply stated, the solution for Cedric and Carolyn was to become intentional about planning a time for their sexual encounters.

Now I realize that some husbands do not like the idea of "planned sex." There are probably several husbands (possibly newlyweds) reading these words who believe their wives begin to tingle when she sees him walking in the door. In his mind, he might be thinking she is craving him all day long. Her yearnings for him finally peak as he walks into the room and touches her shoulder. He may be thinking that as he holds her in his arms, she will proclaim to him her desire for him to throw her to the floor and have his way with her.

Hopefully, this is true for you. However, for most couples, the demands of life and family can negatively impact the best of couples. For the average couple who is seeking to maintain a dynamic sexual relationship, planning is required.

WHY PLAN?

Planning allows you to prioritize what matters. We each have a limited number of days and hours. No one can say yes to everything. Consequently, it is important to live with a mindset where we actively guard our marriage and family by "selective commitments." It is important to acknowledge that when we say yes to one activity, we are saying no to other possibilities. If your family schedule has no room in it for you to be sexually active with your wife, it is time to make some changes.

Planning allows you to filter out the unimportant from the important. If we are not careful "life" will squeeze out the possibilities for sexual intimacy in our marriage. Planning allows us to make a sexual encounter special. Planning is done in recognition that sexual intimacy helps nurture a marriage.

Jesus said, "For what will it profit a man if he gains the whole world, and loses his own soul" (Mark 8:36). Jesus' words point to the vivid truth that certain gains come at a significant cost. Sometimes we lose sight of what is truly important. Your marriage matters. Sexual intimacy is like glue for a marriage. It helps hold it together. It heightens marital satisfaction. I often tell couples that one of the best gifts they can give their children, is for them to see parents who love each other. If sexual intimacy is not a priority, what have we placed above it? What has been gained at its expense?

A Sexual Adventure   83

PLANNING A SEXUAL ENCOUNTER

You may be one of the rare couples who finds no difficulty in maintaining an enthusiastic sexual relationship. However, most couples find that the demands of life (work, children, aging parents, children, sports activities, children, alien encounters and/or children) can choke the life out of a sexual relationship. Most couples can greatly benefit by taking the time "to plan." (I don't want to give the impression that every marital issue can be solved by deciding on a plan to have sex. There can be a host of stressors in life that throw us off balance or make us less than we need to be. However, for a man, sexual frustrations can be a key element impacting his attitude toward his wife. There are a lot of men who believe that "life is grand" when things are going well sexually in their marriage.)

The following is the process I often use when helping a couple plan a sexual encounter. If you are struggling in finding an appropriate time for one another I would encourage you to consider a similar process in planning your "sex life."

Step 1. Decide on the number of sexual encounters that are appropriate for your marriage.
The question I typically ask a couple is:
How often should a married couple with a healthy sexual relationship have sex?

Both husband and wife are asked to respond to the question. In many cases the husband is surprised by his wife's response. After answering the question, I assist the couple in agreeing on what they consider to be a healthy number of sexual encounters for their marriage.

For Carolyn and Cedric, they agreed that for a healthy sexual relationship they should strive to have sex once a week. (Cedric had initially said, "Three times a week," but for a man who was having sex with his wife once every 2 to 3 months, this was a significant and positive change).

Step 2. Decide on the time and place of the sexual encounter.

In deciding when the sexual encounter will occur, it is best to allow the spouse with the lesser sexual desire to give primary feedback. In this case Carolyn picked the day and the time (Sunday at 5pm). Deciding the "when and where" should not be a haphazard decision. The decision requires time and thought. As much as possible, it should be a time when the couple is rested and free of distractions.

Carolyn and Cedric's Decision to Select Sunday at 5pm is Illustrated In the Following Dialogue:

Dan: Carolyn, when would be the best time for you and Cedric to be intimate.

A Sexual Adventure 85

Carolyn: Hmm....there is really not a good time. Mondays through Fridays are pretty hectic.

Dan: You are saying that there is no time available during the work week to be intimate with Cedric.

Carolyn: Not really. By the time I get home I barely have enough time to prepare dinner. Even if we go out to eat, we are both very busy with the children until their bedtime. After the kids go down for bed, I am pretty exhausted. During soccer season we are fortunate to have time to breathe.

Dan: Cedric, is that your opinion as well?

Cedric: She is right. It is tough during the work week to imagine a relaxing evening.

Dan: What about Saturday?

Carolyn: Right now, we are at the soccer field for a large part of the day. When we get back home, I am usually tired. I guess I could see if mom could take the kids home from the field.

Dan: Well, what about Sunday?

Carolyn: After church, Sunday afternoon is my time to clean the house, wash the kids' clothes and try to get ready for the upcoming week.

Dan: Doesn't your mom take the children home with her after church?

Carolyn: Yes, but she does that to free me up to get the house clean, the clothes washed. There is just a lot to do.

Dan: Cedric, what about you? Is your Sunday afternoon hectic?

Cedric: Well ... not really.

Dan: What do you do?

Cedric: I guess... I guess I spend most of it watching sports. It is kind of my only "me time" of the week.

Dan: When do the children come home?

Carolyn: I will usually pick them up after mom feeds them dinner at 6.

Dan: So you pick them up at 7:00?

Carolyn: Usually between 6:30 and 6:45. We try to have them in bed by 7:30.

Dan: Look, if you want to have a healthy sexual relationship, you need be very intentional about it. When the children are older it may be easier. But right now, if the two of you are not careful, you are going to end up with a marriage void of a sex life. Carolyn, is this important to you?

Carolyn: It is ... and I don't want Cedric unhappy.

Dan: Cedric, how important is it to you?

Cedric: Very important!

Dan: Is it important enough that you would spend your Sunday afternoon cleaning the house and washing clothes so Carolyn can rest?

Cedric: I think so

Dan: Is that a yes?

Cedric: Yes, ... yes I can do that.

Dan: With the busy life the two of you live ... and by the way, I am proud of both of you. The service you give to the church. The way you sacrifice time and energy in helping others. The way you love and care for your children. I admire both of you. It is clear that with the busy life you live, from what you have told me, it appears Sunday afternoon is your best opportunity to begin the path towards a healthy sexual relationship. However, for this to occur, and to ensure Carolyn is rested and able to feel she has the time to be sexually intimate, it will require (looking at Cedric) ... you Cedric, to sacrifice your "me time" and clean the house.

Cedric: I can do that.

Carolyn: I can help and still be rested.

Cedric: No... No... I will do it. I can clean and wash clothes. If it will help you be rested for me, ... for us, it is right for me to do it. The truth is, I should have helped you sooner.

Carolyn: (directed towards me, but also reaching over to place her hand on Cedric's hand) He has always been very helpful during the work week. I could not do it without him. He is a great dad.

Cedric: Is there anything else we should decide?

Dan: With any plan there are surprises. A plan is a great step in helping you have a framework to achieve what you want, but even with the best of plans, you need to be prepared for surprises. When things go wrong, ... and they will, don't let it derail you. However, the great news is, there are 52 Sundays in the year. There will be plenty of Sundays this year for things to go right. Cedric, I would also encourage you, that as you work at the house this Sunday, to make sure the bedroom is very clean. You don't want Carolyn lying in bed looking around the room thinking she needs to pick up some clothes.

Carolyn: (To Cedric) Let me do this. I will tidy up our bedroom while you get your shower.

Cedric: That sounds like a great idea.

We continued our session as we dealt with a few other issues. However, in the months ahead Carolyn and

Cedric's plan for sexual intimacy helped energize their marriage and brought an end to a potentially destructive resentment that was beginning to form in Cedric's heart toward his marriage.

A HEALTHY SEX LIFE
(Reviewing A Few Key Points)

1. Be Nice

No, I am not kidding. A wife who is emotionally connected to her husband has an easier time physically connecting with her husband. Being nice and nurturing your wife through your kindness to her is a wonderful path to emotional connections. Conversely, being rude or mean to your wife on a day when you are planning to be sexually intimate with her is a true exercise in futility. You may consider me naive when I say, "Be Nice." However, there are many wives who would be more "in the mood" for sex if their husbands were kind and nurturing.

2. Help Her: "If You Help Us Cook in The Kitchen, We Will Help You Cook in The Bedroom"

During our conferences on "sex" Joyce and I always plan a time when we divide the married couples into groups of "Just Guys" and "Just Girls." The question we ask the groups to answer is: "What Do Husbands/ Wives Need to Know About Sex in Marriage?"

A common response we hear from wives is "a husband who helps his wife around the house, sexually

A Sexual Adventure   91

excites her." This point may be somewhat exaggerated by the women, but the general thought is continually expressed in a variety of ways. The above statement (If you help us cook in the kitchen, we will help you cook in the bedroom) was made at one of our conferences by a lady's group.

Other common answers through the years would be: "There is No Man Sexier Than A Man with A Vacuum Cleaner in His Hand," "Husbands are the Sexiest When They are Holding Their Children's Hands." These answers may be disappointing, but they point to the fact that it is not a husband's "ripped abs" that sexually excites his wife. The Husband who excites his wife is the man who helps her "carry her load" or "cares for and loves what she loves." (This answer, in certain ways, is really a repeat of answer #1 "Be Nice." Yet, its importance is worth repeating.)

3. Follow Her Lead

Some of you have possibly discovered that there are times your wife has a certain sequence in mind on how a sexual encounter will unfold. **CAUTION! If you attempt to alter her plan or make her feel pressured to have sex "outside her sequence" it can turn a potentially exciting evening into a disaster.** Song of Solomon gives us a glimpse into a woman who has a specific sequence in mind.

In Chapter 4 of Song of Solomon, Solomon sounds like a man who is seriously enamored by his bride. He tells her of her beauty. He comments on her eyes, hair, teeth, lips, cheeks, neck, and her breasts. When he tells his bride in Song of Solomon 4:5, "Your two breasts are like two fawns, twins of a gazelle, that graze among the lilies," he sounds like a husband in the mood for sex.

Later in chapter 4, Solomon refers to his bride as a beautiful garden and concludes his comments by stating "Awake, O north wind, and come, O south wind! Blow upon my garden, let its spices flow" (4:16). After these eloquent and somewhat seductive words, the bride responds by stating, "Let my beloved come to his garden, and eat its choicest fruits." Which most husbands would interpret as his wife saying, "Let's have sex!" At this point, even though Solomon sounds like a husband in the mood for sex, something may have happened to delay their union.

In chapter 7 Solomon once again expresses his desire for his bride. He speaks to her of her beauty. He comments on her feet, thighs, navel, belly, breasts, neck, eyes, nose, and head. In verse 7 and following he states, "Your stature is like a palm tree, and your breasts are like its clusters. (8) I say I will climb the palm tree and lay hold of its fruit. Oh, may your breasts be like clusters of the vine, and the scent of your breath like apples, (9) and your mouth like the best wine."

Warning: You are not Solomon. Extreme Caution should be used when commenting on a wife's body parts. Your words should portray love and

adoration. Negative comments or jokes related to your wife's body are unacceptable.

In verse 10 of chapter 7 the bride apparently understands that her groom is in the mood for sex as she states, "I am my beloved's, and his desire is for me." However, it is still not time for sex, because the bride has a romantic stroll into the vineyards in mind. Patience is a virtue, and this groom who is sexually aroused must have a lot of it as he hears his bride say,

> Come my beloved, let us go out into the fields and lodge in the villages; let us go out early to the vineyards and see whether the vines have budded, whether the grape blossoms have opened and the pomegranates are in bloom.
> There I will give you my love.
> Song of Solomon 7:11-12

I seriously question whether any husband, "in the mood for sex" has an iota of concern about "budding vines or blooming pomegranates." However, if the wife has a sequence in mind of what she thinks needs to occur before she "gives herself" to her husband, it is the wise husband who will stay attune to the path she has in mind. As noted previously, to attempt to alter that sequence typically ends in disaster.

4. Don't Rush

Through the years, men have been the brunt of many jokes related to the brevity by which a man makes love. The Pointer Sisters sang a song in the early 1980's entitled "Slow Hand" which points to a woman's need for a man who is not in a hurry to love her.

Many wives would agree with The Pointer Sisters. Making love to your wife is not a race. It is clearly not a time to be checking your watch. Be watchful and take your time in loving your wife.

5. Listen to Your Wife

Try to understand what your wife expects in the bedroom. As a husband you want to hold her in the way she wants to be held. You want to touch her in the way she wants to be touched. Be a quick learner. Remember James 1: 19, "My dear brothers and sisters, take note of this: Everyone should be quick to listen, slow to speak and slow to become angry." These are words of great truth as we enter the bedroom. Listen to your wife. Be attentive to her.

6. Make a Plan

If the pace of life is making it difficult for you to maintain sexual intimacy in your marriage, it is time to make some changes. Your commitment to your wife and to your marriage should be reflected in the manner you SCHEDULE your life. Church commitments, sports events, social gatherings should not be allowed to diminish your relationship with your wife. In yielding your life to Christ, He calls you to keep her a priority. Remember Ephesians 5:25 "Husbands love your wives as Christ loved the church and gave Himself up for her." God gave her you.

You Are Truly
The Main Man in Her Life!

You are the One to Love Her,
Protect Her, Care for Her.

Be The Man and Make A Plan!

Chapter 10
Can We Talk?

Recently, I was counseling with a couple whose morning conversation had escalated from Ben's negative comment about the sausage balls Lisa had prepared for breakfast to threats of divorce and claims as to who would have custody of the children. How is this possible?

The reality is that many couples allow hurts and disagreements to escalate into major confrontations. The situation with Lisa and Ben may seem rather unbelievable. However, it is not. For any couple, faced with a series of stressors in life, a conversation can quickly turn into an unpleasant scene.

Here is a snapshot picture of Ben and Lisa:

Ben and Lisa are a wonderful Christian couple who work together in a family business and try their best to be good parents. Like so many others, with the 2020/2021 pandemic their business was negatively impacted and their financial situation has been somewhat stressful.

Lisa is an amazing young lady with many talents. Two of her passions are sports and cooking. She is known as a great athlete and a great cook. Along with Lisa's love for cooking, she feels a great deal of pride in the food she prepares.

Ben is an outstanding young man. He is well known for excelling in his career. He takes very seriously his role as a dad and as a husband. Unfortunately, along with the decline in their business, Ben fell and injured his shoulder and has not slept well in days.

THE DISPUTE

Lisa woke up early to prepare breakfast for the family, even though she had difficulty sleeping because of Ben's restlessness in bed (he was struggling with shoulder pain and is one who does not like to take pain medication). Unfortunately, both Ben and Lisa state that "yelling and name calling" is their typical manner of dealing with disagreements. They had both learned this style of conflict resolution from their parents.

Due to Lisa's ability in the kitchen, when Ben bit into the sausage ball he was expecting a certain extraordinary taste. His comment upon taking the bite was, "Oh my God Lisa!" From that comment, Lisa reacted with "ugly sarcasm" and the conversation spiraled out of control to the point where Lisa was threatening divorce and Ben was claiming he would gain custody of the children.

Lisa may have overreacted initially, but it is not difficult to understand why Lisa responded so poorly to Ben's comment.

1. Lisa is worried about the family's finances.
2. Lisa's pride in cooking could potentially cause her to be sensitive to criticism.
3. Lisa was physically and mentally vulnerable from her lack of sleep.
4. In spite of a difficult night, Lisa was acting sacrificially in preparing a meal for her family.
5. Lisa was expecting appreciation for her efforts instead of criticism.
6. Yelling is, "What They Do."

In attempting to help Lisa and Ben, we talked about the stressors they were both facing. With the stress of recent events (the pandemic, financial strain, physical pain, lack of sleep, etc.), it was easy to understand how they were both vulnerable to "ugly marital episodes." However, for Ben and Lisa, what helped them most in the weeks after our first meeting was their willingness to work on creating a "New Habit."

LET ME EXPLAIN: NEW HABIT

It is not uncommon for a couple to form habitual patterns in the manner they communicate. Some of you have Google as your default search engine on your computer. Some couples have yelling and screaming as their default in dealing with conflictual issues. Unfortunately, yelling and screaming has zero possibility of reaching a good resolution.

Imagine looking at a dense area of woods with thick underbrush. Only one path has been cut in the underbrush allowing you to enter the woods. The more you enter the path and walk the trail, the easier it becomes to travel the path. Remember, there is only one path into the woods.

When there is already a path cut in the woods, why should a person take the time to make a new path? A new path is often difficult to cut through dense underbrush. If yelling and screaming is your "one path" (your default), it will take commitment, discipline, and time to cut a new path. However, no matter what amount of time and commitment is required, a new path is needed. One person can begin the process, but if both husband and wife agree to work on the path, success will follow.

A tremendous help for a couple attempting to create a new path is for the husband and wife to work together in formulating Rules of Engagement. In fact, this is so important that it is one of the activities that I typically ask couples to complete during marital counseling.

RULES OF ENGAGEMENT

Rules of Engagement are agreements between husband and wife as to what they believe is acceptable in their home when dealing with conflictual issues. (One husband and wife framed their Rules of Engagement and displayed the framed agreement in the entrance foyer of their home.)

Establishing Rules of Engagement is beneficial because both husband and wife have committed to what is permissible and what is not permissible in their home and marriage. Consequently, there is a greater likelihood that some semblance of the rules will be followed when there is a disagreement. For example, even though you may be losing control of your emotions, there is the possibility that your wife still has her emotions "in check" and can proclaim the need for "pausing" until you both have regained your emotional posture. Similarly, in those situations when your wife is losing control, hopefully you are at a point of strength where you can help redeem the moment.

Here is a sample of **Rules of Engagement:**

In Our Home

1. As husband and wife, we will seek to honor Christ in the manner we speak to one another.
2. Profanity or demeaning comments are not allowed in this home.
3. Raised voices are not permitted in this home.

Can We Talk?

4. Respect for one other will be demonstrated in our conversations.
5. A 15-minute pause can be requested at any time.
6. When a person breaks any of the above rules, the person will silence his or her voice.

ASSIGNMENT 1

Together with your wife, formulate Rules of Engagement for your home.

(In addition to asking Ben and Lisa to formulate Rules of Engagement, we also began working on ways to prevent the escalation of their disagreements. The following assignment is often helpful. If escalation is a well-worn path in your marriage it is a worthy exercise.)

ASSIGNMENT 2

Step One

Try to recall the dialogue of a recent disagreement that ended with a poor resolution. You may have to enlist the help of your wife, however, proceed with care and don't allow it to become another fight. If you can't think of one or are concerned it will result in another argument, wait until your next disagreement "that goes bad." As soon as possible after the disagreement, attempt to write out the dialogue that was exchanged. Ask your wife to do the same. If you tell her you are working on being a better husband, she will hopefully be anxious to help. However, if she is suspicious of your intent, just show her this page in the book. The goal is for you to become a better student of the interactions shared between you and your wife. The goal is to become a man who can redeem moments between husband and wife.

Note: It is difficult for some couples to agree on the dialogue that has occurred between them. If that is an issue, use your phone to record your conversations with your wife when you are discussing conflictual issues (your wife needs to agree to this).

I realize some couples are resistant to a recording of their disagreements, believing a recorder is too intrusive. Nonetheless, many couples have found a

The goal is to become a man who can redeem moments between husband and wife.

recorder to be helpful. Truly, any negative feelings about using "voice memos" on your phone to record your conversations should pale in comparison to the possibility of enhancing your ability to have a conversation with good resolution. Hopefully, as you develop your "intervention skills" your children will be freed from the possibility of hearing what you or your wife did not want to record. Another benefit of a recorder is its ability to help us hear how we sound when we are discussing

Can We Talk?

conflictual issues. Some couples are surprised to hear words that they did not remember saying, and the use of tones, they can't believe came from their mouths.

If you and your wife have a tendency to allow your conversations to severely escalate in volume, I would encourage the use of a recorder. Otherwise, the likelihood of writing out an accurate dialogue between you and your wife is extremely unlikely.

Step Two

Look over the dialogue with your wife and attempt to find places where the disagreement can be re-directed toward a better resolution. Consider ways the conversation can be redeemed. This is strategic planning. With focus and effort, a couple can make great strides in becoming a student of their conversations with one another and experience success in curbing escalation.

I have had couples admit to me that even in the middle of a fight, there was a strong longing to end the disagreement and be at peace with each other. However, they just didn't feel the freedom to do it. A disagreement does not have to escalate out of control. Truly, some couples by the use of an "emergency word or signal" have learned how to derail a disagreement that was headed for an awful conclusion.

As a husband, instead of being a part of the problem, be a part of the solution. "Can We Talk" parts 2 and 3, will also be helpful to you if you are seeking to gain better control over your interactions with your wife.

Chapter 11
Can We Talk? Part II

Both you and your wife will occasionally say things that will be perceived by the other as hurtful. Everyone is going to have a bad day. The question is, when your wife is less than the person she should be, who are you? When your wife says or does something that qualifies as mean or harsh, what do you do? A common response to a hurtful statement is to attempt to hurt the other person in return.

When Ben took a bite out of the sausage ball Lisa had prepared, his comment, "Oh my God, Lisa" was probably not his best moment. Many couples allow hurt feelings to take them on a rocky path of accusations, complaints and defensive posturing. When your wife reacts to what you consider, "An Innocent Comment," can you avoid the cascading emotional wreckage that could potentially occur?

> **When your wife is less than the person she should be, who are you?**

DON'T PLAY THE GAME

As we noted with Lisa and Ben, couples will often find their way to words which carry the most impact. Without question, divorce and child custody are extremely powerful words. Do you remember the boxing game, "Rock'Em Sock'Em Robots"? The purpose of the game was to knock the head off of your opponent.

Even though you are not physically knocking the head off your wife, if you are not careful, you can easily participate in allowing a disagreement to spiral into an exchange of verbal punches where each person is attempting to achieve a "knockout punch." Without a diversion tactic or intentional intervention, disagreements can become quite unpleasant. We gravitate towards words that harm and wound. These "power words" are our attempt to impact the other person. We use words that will make the other person know how serious we are about the current situation. We search for the word or phrase that will have "knock out" power, buckling our spouse's knees and forcing them to retreat to his or her corner of the ring.

ADVOID BEING M.A.D.

Words that may be used to maim, kill and destroy are words that should be removed from our marital vocabulary. During the cold war there was a phrase, "Mutually Assured Destruction," which recognized the nuclear abilities of Russia and the United States to destroy one another. The phrase Mutually Assured Destruction conveyed the belief that if either country attacked the other country with nuclear weapons, through nuclear attack and nuclear counterattack, both countries would be annihilated. The belief that the use of nuclear weapons would result in the annihilation of the country who initiated the attack was an extremely strong deterrent for nuclear warfare. It would not be sensible for a country to attack another country if the end result would be its own annihilation.

In the same way, it isn't logical for a husband to continue to engage in a heated exchange with his wife while he is holding the nuclear launch codes and ready to fire. The result of his attack would be clear, Mutually Assured Destruction. For a husband's own sake, and the well-being of his wife, caution must be exercised. The words coined by Shakespeare, "Discretion is the better part valor" are fitting.

Truly, there are certain words or phrases used by husbands and wives which we should list under the category of M.A.D. and exclude from our marriages. Without question, words are powerful. Have you ever been walking along, feeling great? The sky is blue and there is a refreshing breeze on your face. Maybe, you are singing a little song. Suddenly, you are blindsided, and someone comes up to you and says something that cuts to the very core of your being. If you did not know better, you would have thought someone stuck you with a knife and you feel as if the blood is draining from your body. How could such a wonderful day turn so quickly to a day of woe and misery? Scripture states it well, "Death and life are in the power of the tongue" (Proverbs 18:21).

A GOOD WORD

Just as there are words which should be removed from our marital vocabulary, there are other words which should be added to our daily dialogue with our spouse. As harsh words bruise our spirits, a good word can brighten our day. Listen to how scripture proclaims the value of words.

Proverbs 16:24 "Kind words are like honey, sweet to the soul and healthy for the body."
Proverbs 18:4 "A person's words can be life-giving water..."

With spoken and written word, be a person who breathes life into your wife through your words.

(Some husbands and wives are not comfortable verbally communicating sincere feelings. If you find it challenging to express yourself verbally, don't forget the power of a handwritten note. Text messages are great compliments, but please also consider using pen and paper when it's time to share some serious feelings. A text message will be deleted in 6 months, but a letter will live in a secret dresser drawer and may be read time and again.)

A FILTER BEFORE YOUR MOUTH

As we have mentioned, there are words you should not say. These words are harmful to your wife and can potentially destroy your marriage. Conversely, there are words that are important and meaningful to your wife. **These words can nurture your wife and strengthen your marriage.**

Your grandmother may have told you, "If you can't say something nice, don't say anything at all." No doubt, a husband who is seeking to "Be Nice" to his wife utilizes care in the manner he speaks to his wife. Ephesians 4:29 is a great verse for a husband to use as a filter for his words as he speaks to his wife.

Ephesians 4:29 **proclaims, "Let no unwholesome word proceed from your mouth but only such a word as is good for edification, according to the need of the moment, so that it will give grace to those who hear."**

A GREAT VERSE

Ephesians 4:29 is a tremendous verse for each of us! Truly, it presents some great guidelines to help us "Be Nice" as we speak to our wife.

1. Speak no unwholesome word to your wife.
2. Speak words of edification to your wife.
3. Speak according to the needs of your wife.
4. Speak words that "give grace" to your wife.

For 40 years, I have used this verse to guide my words with Joyce and to convict me of wrong when I have verbally messed up. If you and I can be faithful in our obedience to this one verse, I believe we have taken a significant step in being a husband who loves his wife by his words and is pleasing in God's sight.

SPEAK NO UNWHOLESOME WORD TO YOUR WIFE

Ephesians 4:29 "Let no unwholesome word proceed from your mouth...."

The verse is clear. A husband should not have unwholesome words coming from his mouth. It is of interest that the Greek word translated "unwholesome" is only used 8 times in 6 different verses in the entire New Testament (Matthew 7:17,18; Matthew 12:33; Matthew 13:48; Luke 6:43; Ephesians 4:29).

In the passages in Matthew and Luke, (except for Matthew 13:48) the Greek word refers to a fruit tree that has gone bad and to the bad fruit it produces. In Matthew 13:48 the Greek word refers to bad fish that need to be thrown out. It is not fit for human consumption. Are there words used in your home that are "not fit for use"? Are there words coming from your mouth that need to be discarded? There should be "no room" for unwholesome words in your home.

MISSION

Objective:
Discard inappropriate words from your life.

Details:
Prayerfully consider the words you use when speaking to your wife. If there are words which are inappropriate (MAD) or unfit for human consumption, it is time to begin the work of discarding them from your life.

Discuss with your wife these words and phrases which should not be a part of your marital vocabulary. Make an agreement with your wife to ban (to the best of your ability) these words and phrases from your home (you may want to add these words to your Rules of Engagement).

SPEAK WORDS OF EDIFICATION TO YOUR WIFE
Ephesians 4:29 "...but only such a word that is good for edification..."

What word does your wife long to hear in her life? What words are most meaningful to her? As you know, the word edification means to build up. For many a wife, there is probably not a huge number of people in her life who have lined up to tell her that she is wonderful, awesome, and a person of great beauty. Too often we are met at work and home with criticism, judgement, and additional expectations. Words of praise are not a daily experience for many of us. As a husband, you must recognize your responsibility to speak words into your wife's life that build her up.

In the series of movies entitled *Mission Impossible* there is always a high-tech device that describes to Tom Cruise his new mission. During the "presentation" it states, "Your mission, should you choose to accept it." Your wedding day may not have had the "action scenes" present in *Mission Impossible*, but you also have been presented with an awesome mission. On the day you said, "I do," you accepted the very blessed mission of being The Man in your wife's life to bring a word that will build her up. No one else has this call on his life as you, ... and fortunately this message will not destruct in 5 seconds.

MISSION

Objective

Actively engage in speaking words of encouragement into your wife's life.

Details

Ask your wife what words or phrases are most meaningful to her. You might simply hand her an index card where along the top of it you have written, "Words I

Love to Hear," asking her to respond when she has opportunity. If she is hesitant to respond, as previously stated, tell her this is done in your attempt to be the husband God is calling you to be. After she has completed her list, if there are any words or phrases that are a surprise or confusing to you, ask your wife to tell you why that word or phrase is so meaningful to her.

Now, place this index card in your wallet. Your mission is to be the husband that daily speaks words of edification into his wife's life. With your list of words and phrases that are important to your wife, begin incorporating these words into your conversations with your wife. You may want to periodically whisper them in her ear, write them on notes you leave strategically around the house, or shout them out as you are walking with her down "Main Street." Do whatever is most appropriate to the moment. Do whatever you believe would be most meaningful to her. **Be the Man!**

SPEAK ACCORDING TO HER NEEDS
Ephesians 4:29. "...according to the need of the moment..."

These seven words in verse 29 are extremely meaningful, "according to the need of the moment." The mere wording of the phrase implies a knowledge of what is occurring in another person's life. If you are not aware of what is taking place in your wife's life, how can you address the needs of her life? The phrase "according to the need of the moment" indicates a continual awareness. This is like the watchman who is ever vigilant to make sure the area before him is safe. You are the watchman in your wife's life. You are to be vigilant in your awareness of what is taking place in her life. There will be times in her life where her work, or the kids, or other family/friend issues, may overwhelm her. According to the needs of her day, you need to be the man who can encourage her in words, and comfort her with an embrace, helping her know she is safe in your care.

MISSION

Objective

Engage in active listening with your wife.

Details

Schedule times when you are available to listen to your wife. Too often when wives start sharing, men start interrupting with solutions as they attempt to "fix things." In this moment, your job is to listen and to be empathetic. You are primarily a mirror. You are a sounding board, repeating back to her the statement that she has made to you, as you ensure her that you are listening to her. If you ask a question, it is to clarify…it is to help you gain a clearer understanding of a statement she has made to you.

SPEAK WORDS OF GRACE
TO YOUR WIFE

Ephesians 4:29, "...so that it will give grace to those who hear."

You have possibly heard a preacher proclaim that the word "mercy" refers to you not receiving the punishment from God you deserve. In that same statement the preacher may have said, "The word 'Grace' refers to us receiving from God what we don't deserve." Grace is often interpreted within the context of forgiveness.

In the letter to the Ephesians the Greek word for grace (transliterated charis) is used 12 times (Ephesians 1:2,6,7; 2:5,7,8; 3:2,7,8; 4:7,29; 6:24). As you read through these verses the use of the word implies more than just forgiveness. Ephesians 1:7 makes this clear, "In Him we have redemption through His blood, the forgiveness of our trespasses, according to the riches of His grace." Thus, in Ephesians 1:7 we see references to both... God's Forgiveness, as well as the riches of God's Grace. Consequently, the word "Grace" seems to refer to something more than forgiveness.

I believe the word Grace refers to God's powerful movement of redeeming love in our life. With this in mind it seems appropriate to conclude that in verse 29 God's Word is proclaiming that we should speak in a manner that Redeeming Love is experienced by the hearer of our words.

Can We Talk? Part II   115

You and I should speak to our wives in such a manner that our words are loving and redemptive. Our words to our wives should be words of life. This is the end result of guarding our mouths from unwholesome comments, and speaking words of edification, especially in those moments of great need.

MISSION

Objective

Memorize Ephesians 4:29 and seek to embrace this verse as a "life verse" to hold before your life (and mouth).

"Let no unwholesome word proceed from your mouth, but only such a word as is good for edification, according to the need of the moment, so that it will give grace to those who hear" (Ephesian 4:29).

Chapter 12
Can We Talk? Part III: Stop Yelling

You may think it odd I have entitled this chapter Stop Yelling. I do so because I literally hear it occurring in far too many homes. From the sweet "church lady" teaching in the children's area, to the minister admired by all, I am aware of many fine men and women who have given themselves permission to yell and scream. It really needs to stop.

> We need to put an end
> to yelling in our homes.

I believe at least 75 percent of Christian couples "yell" at one another in their homes. Years ago, I would not have made this statement. However, after being surprised on numerous occasions by couples I would have labeled the "sweetest couple," it appears to be true.

I know of couples who have the friendliest voice-mails. If you call their cell phones, the voicemail has comments like, "God loves you so much and so do I." Yet, they totally lose control when they disagree with one another. Children have spoken to me about their fathers, leaders in the church, who cuss their moms and scream profanity at the children. I know of sweet ladies who are so sweet a room smells better from their presence. Nonetheless, in my office, I have heard and seen them filet the flesh off of their husbands. (You might think it odd that a couple would actually scream in my office, but it is a reality. No one has ever been shot; however, one wife did break a few bones in her hand as she was swinging to hit her husband and inad-vertently hit the metal doorframe in my office.)

If you allow yelling in your home, it is time for a **change!**

I have been singing a song with my granddaugh-ter with the lyrics "the wheels on the bus go around and round." The imagery from the words seem to imply that everything is going well. The bus is moving, the wheels are turning, it sounds like it is going to be a good day. Unfortunately, there are days when very few things are going right. There are days when it feels as if the wheels on the bus have fallen off and dark clouds have encompassed our life.

I regularly encounter couples whose wheels have come off their bus. They might sit in my office in silence, reminiscent of those who have lost all hope. They may spend the majority of the time screaming at each other. Many times, it is a wonderful and precious couple where neither the husband nor wife are to blame for the mishaps in their lives. However, both husband and wife having reached the breaking point and full of emotions, find the easiest target to be the marriage mate.

Tragically, as previously noted, there are many husbands who view their marriage partner as the safest avenue to vent the frustrations of the day. It is as if there is the belief that a husband can treat his wife any way he wants to without cost. Similarly, there is the belief that unkind actions and spiteful words towards a wife can be distributed without consequences. A husband might say to himself, "If I yell at my boss I might get fired. If I 'act out' in public I might be arrested. However, ugliness towards a wife in the privacy of my home...no problem."

What should you do if you have reached the point in your relationship where attempts at communication have spiraled out of control and daily yelling matches are the norm? The answer seems evident. Unfortunately, I am aware that some husbands do not sense the need to alter the manner they express themselves to their wife. I have had individuals tell me that "yelling" is just the way they "do things." I have been

> **There is a belief that unkind words towards a wife can be distributed without consequence.**

told by others that they are simply from a loud family and they are continuing the family legacy.

Recognizing that there are those who feel it is okay to continue the pattern of yelling or screaming at their wives, I want to offer an opposing position. Consequently, in this chapter I offer a few more words of warning against yelling, and some thoughts which I hope will motivate and encourage others on how to begin to work towards creating a home void of yelling.

THOU SHALL NOT YELL

When God was dealing with His people in the Old Testament, He felt it wise to help them know how to "live well" by giving Moses the Ten commandments. If I was tasked with the responsibility of compiling the 10 commandments of marriage, at least one of those would be the commandment, "Thou Shall Not Yell."

As noted previously, I realize that some men think "yelling" does not matter. Their life verse is probably James 3:8 "But no man can tame the tongue," and so they have decided there is no need to try. In fact, I am very aware of guys who will "yell it out" with the wife, feel much better getting that out of their system or "off their chest," and 10 minutes later they will ask the wife if she is in the mood for sex (in case you are not aware, yelling at your wife is not beneficial to your sex life).

At this point, it should be clear I am extremely opposed to "Yelling" in the home. Nonetheless, let me present several additional reasons you should not allow it in your home.

SEVEN REASONS "THOU SHALL NOT YELL"

1. It is sin.

Yelling creates a barrier between you and God. Truly, in the letter of James we hear strong words against the person who does not control his tongue. James 1:26 states "If anyone considers himself religious and yet does not keep a tight rein on his tongue, he deceives himself and his religion is worthless."

Thankfully, our God is a merciful God who forgives us when we confess our "vocal blunders" to Him. However, I do believe this verse (James 1:26) helps us understand how our testimony can be damaged when our words, or the manner we express our self "in word," does not give evidence of our relationship with Jesus.

2. When a husband is yelling at his wife, there is the strong possibility he will say something harmful to her.

Many people deal poorly with conflictual issues. As emotions start elevating, and those in conflict start raising their voices, facts are no longer relevant. The goal for many shifts from dealing with issues, to proclaiming some word that is hurtful to the other person.

It is hard to comprehend the long-term impact of toxic (radioactive) materials. It is claimed Chlorine-36 has a half-life of 300,000 years and Neptunium-237, a half-life of 2 million years. However, many of you are aware of the harmful effect of toxic words. It is impossible to place a "half-life" on their influence in our lives. Without question, they can "diminish-life" far beyond the time it takes for the words to be spoken. Unfortunately, the impact of certain words can linger in our hearts and minds for months, years and sometimes a lifetime.

Can you recall words that were spoken to you that have had a lasting impact? We need to be careful with our words.

3. Yelling is a poor testimony to children and other family members and friends.

I often tell young dads that they should not pick up anything in their hands they are not prepared to place in someone else's hand. I will warn them, "If you have it in your hand, you need to be prepared to hand it to your children. Because one day, due to you holding in your hand, there is a strong likelihood it will be in their hands."

The same is true for the words that come from your mouth. If there are words you do not want your child to speak, you need to filter those words from your mouth. As has been said many times, there is no significant weight or meaning to the phrase, "Do as I say and not as I do."

> **The impact of certin words can linger in our hearts and minds for a lifetime.**

4. When a husband yells, he may have shifted from the rational part of his brain. (You may become careless and irrational in your words and not even realize it.)

Did you know that when an interaction between husband and wife escalates to yelling, it is possible that both husband and wife have stopped using the "thinking part" of the brain? This is one of the reasons we are prone to make statements that are harmful to each other.

I have asked my wife Joyce, to share with you the physiology of what takes place in the brain as an argument escalates. Joyce is a beautiful and awesome lady. She taught anatomy and physiology many years in the public school. One of her primary focuses, when we speak at marriage enrichment conferences, is to educate husbands and wives on how human anatomy influences our marriage relationship. She shares about the physiology of relationships in our upcoming book *A*

Guide to a Good Marriage: Sex and the Christian Couple.
I believe what she has to say is quite extraordinary.

> **Dan**: Joyce, is this true? Is it true that in an argument, as the argument escalates, a person will typically stop using the rational part of the brain?

> **Joyce**: Yes, I know this may sound strange, and it is probably difficult for some to believe but you are exactly right. The reality is, if a husband and wife are arguing and the dispute has escalated to where they are yelling at each other, it is most likely that neither one of them is using the thinking part of the brain. This is usually shocking for most people. To help us understand let me present the basics of how the brain processes messages during stressful altercations.

> During times of danger, the body is designed to react quickly for protection from the perceived source of danger. This reaction, which you have probably heard of, is called the "fight or flight" reflex. This is an automatic reflex. When danger or some threatening event occurs, the control center for words and actions shifts from the cerebrum, the thinking part of the brain, to a part of the brain

called the amygdala. It is the amygdala, that initiates the "fight or flight" reaction during times of perceived danger. It can also occur when experiencing emotions such as anger, anxiety and fear. In a way, the amygdala sounds a physiological alarm when activated.

Dan: If a tiger was in the room, it would occur?

Joyce: Right

Dan: Or a fox?

Joyce: Yes

Dan: I think you're a fox.

Joyce: Thank you, but please let me continue.

Dan: OK

Joyce: The "fight or flight" reflexive response causes a person to experience increased heart rate, increased blood pressure, and the eye pupils to dilate. These responses are preparing the body to react quickly to flee from or confront the "dangerous enemy."

Dan: I am not going to say anything.

Joyce: You already have.... As I was saying, the amygdala sounds a physiological alarm when activated, keying what has been termed the "fight or flight" response. This is very effective if you are dealing with a tiger in the room. However, the "fight or flight" response is not an effective way to communicate with your wife, who I am sure is very precious and clearly not a dangerous enemy. Nevertheless, in an argument when there is heightened emotional stress, the amygdala hijacks the response process from the rational part of the brain. Unfortunately, if one speaks without using the thinking part of the brain, it is possible that words will be said that were never meant to be said.

It is also worthwhile to note that it is in the amygdala that emotional memories are stored. Consequently, in the midst of an escalating argument, you have not only shifted from the rational part of the brain, but to add to the present dilemma, the part of the brain that is taking control, contains a host of emotional memories. Memories which can potentially be used to harm your wife. To avoid this dangerous scenario,

James 1:18 provides direction to help us communicate with thoughtful responses: **"My dear brothers and sisters, take note of this: Everyone should be quick to listen, slow to speak and slow to become angry."**

We would be wise to follow the instructions from God's Word. Being attentive to God's Word will help prevent an amygdala hijacking. Consequently, during times of anger and stress, you and I should slow down and allow the information to go to the thinking part of the brain. In doing this, a righteous response can be formulated. The thinking part of the brain allows us to evaluate feelings and stay calm. It also helps us to more effectively read each other's non-verbal communications.

Dan: It sounds similar to what my mom told me to do if I am ever on fire. She said, "You need to stop, drop, and roll."

Joyce: No, I don't think that relates at all. It would be difficult to talk to you while you are rolling around on the floor. However, this is really quite important. By pausing and allowing time for the thinking part of the brain to process information, a person can carefully choose words that need to be said and refrain from saying words that are best left unsaid. In addition, during the thinking process, a person can begin to recognize patterns of behavior that have developed and identify new patterns that need to be initiated.

When you look at the body and the way God made us, it is important to be faithful in treating one another in a way that honors Him. Understanding how God made us, clearly points out that we were not made to verbally abuse each other. The fact that when an argument escalates to yelling, we shift from the rational part of the brain, is a clear indicator that we have detoured from God's plan for us. Nothing good comes from such activity. How can a husband believe he can reach a good solution when he is not using the rational part of his brain?

Again, God's Word is clear, we should be "Quick to Listen and Slow to speak." This creates the potential for better solutions and better behavior. I think it positions a husband and wife to truly experience the joy that God desires to indwell each marriage.

Dan: Thank you, Joyce. You are very sweet, a lot of fun, and I love you.

5. Yelling does not produce solutions.

As noted previously, from the point yelling begins, dialogue that can bring a clearer understanding of the issues involved in a dispute has ended.

6. Yelling is self-indulgent.

A few years ago, Joyce and I were speaking at a Marriage Conference in North Carolina and I stated my opposition to yelling and the concerns I have over allowing it to continue in a home. After the conference, a lady walked up to me and handed me a folded piece of paper. On the paper was written a note that stated, "I yell at my husband in my home because I feel safe."

I realize that "feeling safe" may sound like a good rational for yelling and I am glad this lady feels safe. I do have to wonder how safe her husband feels. I did not see him. He may have been locked up in the trunk of their car.

Unfortunately, as I have mentioned, it is not uncommon for the "yeller" to think there is nothing wrong with yelling. As noted, in some cases I have had individuals express the belief that it makes them feel better. Sadly, in the past 30 years I have worked with many families who are emotionally struggling, and I am very aware of the feelings of children and youth who have experienced the "joy of screaming parents." I have never encountered a child whose screaming parent helped the child feel safe (or better).

It is wonderful that the lady who was yelling at her husband felt safe and secure in her home.

Nevertheless, yelling is oppressive in a home. It undermines the sense of safety and security for the children. It fosters an atmosphere of fear.

For every husband or wife who feels good because he or she just had "a good yell," there is at least one other person sick to his or her stomach and struggling to fall asleep. For every person that feels safe to yell in the home, there is the strong possibility that he or she is creating a home that does not feel safe for anyone else. Truly, yelling compromises the safety and security of any home.

7. Yelling undermines trust in a relationship.

Josh was a very private person. He said he had always been hesitant to open up to anyone about his childhood, or the pain he had experienced in his life. After marrying Janet, he was encouraged to see the marriage relationship as his safe haven. With the encouragement from his best friend, he began sharing with his wife some of the deep hurts he had experienced as a child.

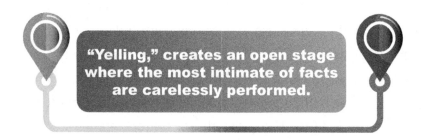

"Yelling," creates an open stage where the most intimate of facts are carelessly performed.

One of the more "raw" and tender seasons of Josh's life pertained to the painful memories he had regarding his dad. His dad was always very critical of him and would regularly tell Josh that "he was worthless

SEVEN REASONS "THOU SHALL NOT YELL"

1. It is sin
2. When a husband is yelling at his wife, he will likely say something harmful
3. Yelling is a poor testimony to family and friends
4. When yelling begins, You are in the process of shifting from the part of the brain which enables rational conversation.
5. Yelling does not produce solutions
6. Yelling is self-indulgent
7. Yelling undermines trust

and would never amount to anything." Josh told Janet that he continues to struggle with those thoughts even today.

One day Josh and Janet were arguing. The disagreement had escalated to the point where they were verbally out of control and saying some very harsh statements to one another. Josh had just made a comment about Janet's weight that was extremely insensitive and hurtful to her and he was "one up" in the fight. Suddenly, Janet found herself making a comment, she could not believe was coming from her mouth. She would later say she did not mean to say it. She said, "It just came out." Nonetheless, Janet screamed at Josh, "You know, your dad was right, you never will amount to anything!"

In that moment, part of Josh's heart closed to Janet as he realized that there was a danger in trusting her with the most intimate parts of his life. Josh now faced the horrible realization that hurts from his past, shared with Janet would be used by her to hurt him. With 12 words (spoken in approximately 4 seconds) she had torn down a bridge between them that would take years to rebuild.

Proverbs 11:29 "He who brings trouble on his family will inherit only wind...the fool who provokes his family to anger and resentment will finally have nothing worthwhile left..."

THE MOUTH THAT CAN'T BE CONTROLLED

Now I realize there are some very fine men of God who are thinking, "It just doesn't seem like I can control my outbursts directed at my wife." Let me ask you to please try. In previous chapters we have already addressed some tools that should be helpful to you. Let's review.

EIGHT DIRECTIVES TO CONTROL YOUR MOUTH

1. Label yelling as unacceptable in your home.

Make a Covenant between husband and wife that "yelling" will not be a part of your marriage. (If you developed "Rules of Engagement," this would be included in those rules.)

As mentioned, if husband and wife have agreed that yelling at each other in the home is wrong, even though one person loses control, there is the possibility that the other spouse will still have the ability to stop the couple from engaging in an emotional "free fall." With your wife's help, you can bring an end to your yelling. Everything will not change overnight. It might but it will probably require time and a few "ReDos," as you stop old habits and start new ones.

I must admit, I am continually amazed at a person's ability to control and direct his or her verbal expressions. I was with a couple, a very nice couple. They are always talking to people about Jesus. Unfortunately, they were having a disagreement over the way the husband had spent their tax refund money and asked me to come to their home to tell the other spouse that he/she was wrong.

I am not exaggerating when I say that being with them was like grabbing hold of the back end of a roller coaster. Both of them would start screaming, and then calm down, and start screaming again. It was a wild ride.

At one point, the wife went into a verbal tirade of such severity, I was surprised the husband had any skin left on his body. Truly, it was "Really Bad!" From her facial contortions to her arm and hand gestures, it was astonishing that such a nice person could express herself in such a horrible manner. Admittedly, her robust ability to use foul language was remarkable. I am fairly confident it would take a great deal of practice to put together as many profane and hurtful words in one sentence as she did (or she was naturally gifted with the ability to verbally slay someone). However, right after one of her verbal tirades, she looked at me and put her hands up to her face. Holding the palms of her hands to her chin she proclaimed in this sweet and sincere voice, "Pastor Dan, I just hate you seeing me like this."

Proverbs 30:32 "If you have played the fool and exalted yourself ..if you have planned evil...clap your hands over your face."

You have probably seen this type of metamorphosis before. A person is out of control towards someone and then in the next moment, he or she is kind to someone else. I was in the cafeteria at Emory Hospital, sitting at a table close to a mom and her 3 children. I am sure she must have been stressed because she was verbally assaulting her children.

I was about to speak to her when her phone rang, and with this pleasant voice she began talking to whoever had called her. I was thankful that she and the children could have a calmer moment. Nonetheless, how is it possible a person can be at a level that appears to be out of control and then suddenly change into this "sweet talking person"? At some level, I think it relates to what we allow ourselves to do.

The couple with the money dispute is a notable example. (The lady with the natural gift to "verbally slay.") If the wife had put half of the energy she used to be so humble to me, and had directed it towards her husband, they probably would not have needed me. I believe she had given herself permission to talk "any way she wanted" to her husband. I believe the husband had given himself permission to talk "any way he wanted" to his wife.

Have you given yourself permission to talk "any way you want"… to express anything you are feeling, to your wife? If so, you need to stop. You need to label your home as the place where yelling is not permitted--the place where you seek to carry the best of who you are to your wife. This is not saying you cannot share "your feelings" with you wife. However, if sharing your feelings and opinions with your wife is leaving her bruised and broken, you have crossed over into an area which is inappropriate for a husband who is seeking to love and care for his wife.

(And yes, if you are wondering, I did try to help the couple with money issues realize what you already know. The most important challenge they were facing was not how they spend money. The more important issue was how they treated each other. What about you? If someone offered you some money to be mean and hateful to your wife, would you take the offer? Would it be worth ten dollars for every tear that you can make drop from her eyes, twenty dollars if you can bruise her spirits, or one hundred dollars if you can make her question her value or worth? I've seen couples argue, claw, fight and scream over such small sums of money but the truth is, money is rarely the "real issue.")

You say you can't stop Yelling ...

2. Go to school:

Become a student of your "Yelling Episodes."

a. Be honest with yourself and examine what takes place in your dialogue with your wife that results in the loss of verbal control. What was the issue involved? Is this a reoccurring disagreement? What is the time of day? What was said by who and who was the first to lose control and why did this occur? Look for repeating patterns.

b. If there is a certain situation that seems to ignite you and your wife, replay the situation and establish some new scenarios that don't involve screaming.

When football teams scrimmage, they often run the same play over and over so that in the game situation, they have a play that carries them over the goal line. In a similar way, prepare your mind for ways you and your wife can "win" in your conversations with each other.

3. TOP (Time Out Please):

If your conversation takes a turn onto "Yell At You Boulevard," call a time out.

Together with your wife, select a "word" or phrase that signals it is time to stop talking and go to your separate corners. Consider for your "TOP," a neutral phrase like "Blue Herring." You probably know, but phrases like ... "Shut Up, Shut your Mouth, Shut your Yapper, or Stifle yourself Up," are typically not good ones to use. If you don't want to use a word, maybe you can agree on a simple signal (waving a white flag) to let your wife know you are about to become a person who is less than the man God wants you to be ... and that you really need to take a break.

I met with a young couple that began working to gain emotional control of their relationship a year ago. Unfortunately, it was reaching the point where she (not the guy) was becoming physical with her husband. Thankfully, within only a month they were able to make great strides in regaining control of how they treated one another. One evening the wife called and said they had an issue where they were about to lose it, and she was calling me to see if I could meet with them that week to help them work through the disagreement. I asked her if they needed to meet that evening and she said, "No, we agreed to 'put a pin in it' and wait until we see you."

In the months ahead the agreement to "put a pin in it" became their way of agreeing to end a conversation that was going off course, enabling them to discuss it at a later time when they were in a better place emotionally to handle the conversation. Couples can regain control of their lives. For this couple, the TOP that worked was to simply "put a pin in it." Find what works for you and your wife.

Pro Tip: If you are struggling with deciding the point at which a conversation is "too hot to handle" try the following. Hold hands with your wife, and as long as you can gently hold hands you can talk with one another. The moment you feel hands being squeezed or the need to pull your hand away from your wife you need to stop talking. If you can't gently hold hands, you can't talk.

EIGHT DIRECTIVES TO CONTROL YOUR MOUTH

1. Label yelling as unacceptable
2. Go to school
3. TOP (Time Out Please)
4. Let's get physical
5. Touch
6. Phone-a-Friend
7. Write out your statements to each other
8. When you are vulnerale .... try to avoid confictual issues

**Let Each Of Us Strive
To Be A Husband
Who Brings A Gentle Answer.**

4. Let's get physical:

When you find yourself losing control, stop talking and do an activity that is physically demanding.

Go for a long walk. If it is not possible to walk together, do so separately. If it is raining outside, go up and down the stairs in your house until you are totally exhausted.

5. Touch:

Go to bed with your body in contact with your wife's body.

There is something soothing about human touch. An embrace can bring comfort in the midst of the most difficult of days. God made us in such an extraordinary manner, that the human body can respond in a unique way when it is in contact with another person. When you make skin to skin contact with your wife, the hormone oxytocin is emitted in the body. Oxytocin has been called (among other names) the love hormone, trust hormone and attachment hormone. If you are at a point of deep frustrations due to your inability to deal with a situation, (at bedtime) try lying next to your wife and simply ask if you can hold her. It is quite possible that you and your wife will wake up in a better mood and more enabled to control your tongues, because you spent time being in contact with this precious person God has gifted to you.

6. Phone-a-Friend:

Ask a trusted friend to help hold you accountable (in being a person who guards his words). In the first months of a couple training themselves to "live in control of their mouths," I ask the couple to call me if they believe a disagreement is causing them to become too emotional. Just the act of allowing someone else into your life for accountability can be quite helpful. What you don't want to do is to stay hidden behind the doors of your home.

7. Write out your statements to each other:

In this approach, talking is not allowed. In dealing with an emotional issue, your entire dialogue is written out (most likely on an iPad, iPhone, or computer). There is value in writing your thoughts out. It allows you to take the needed time to clearly express yourself. Even though emotional reactions can be expressed in written form, interchanges are less likely to contain careless reactionary expressions.

8. When you are vulnerable .... try to avoid conflictual issues:

You know yourself and your limitations. There are some who do not play well with others when they are tired, or hungry, or burdened by some other issue at work. If extraneous issues have compromised your ability to be at your best, please recognize this is not the best moment to try to solve a problem between you and your wife. As much as possible, (for you to maintain emotional strength) you need to be well fed, rested, and free of other burdens when attempting to resolve marital disagreements.

Chapter 13
I've Fallen & She Won't Let Me Up

I hope your marriage is one that is satisfying and a true blessing in your life. However, let us suppose that in the last several years you have become a little negligent and your marriage is not what it should be today. Maybe your wife has expressed discontent. She may have said, for the sake of the children she will stay in the marriage, but that she does not love you. She might have said, she will always love you, but she is not "in love" with you. She may have told you, "I am done, I am through."

In your effort to restore the marriage, you have read this book and for the last several weeks you have made a real effort to be nice to your wife. However, there does not seem to be any change on her part. You had hoped for "better."

Recently, I received a voicemail stating that unless I paid some delinquent bill, police authorities would come to my house to arrest me. I did not respond. I am presently not in jail. (There was no delinquent bill and the police never came to my home.)

Today I received a phone call stating that my Social Security number had been canceled because of suspicious activity by someone using my social security number who claimed to be me. I did not respond. Guess what, my Social Security number was not canceled.

Through the years I have received numerous messages that were from people, (quoting Will Ferrell from the movie *Elf*) "Sitting on a throne of lies!"

The Bottom Line:
Sometimes it is Hard to Trust What Someone is Saying.

If you have spent a lot of time disappointing your wife in the past, she is expecting you to disappoint her now. Even though she sees you trying, mentally she is saying to herself, "Sure, he is doing this now, but the moment I give in and say everything is ok, he will go back and act like he did in the past."

There are times a man has to prove himself. The sincerity of what you are doing and the ability for you to regain your wife's trust in "The New You," will require Consistent Action Over Time (CAOT). No matter how she acts or responds, you need to be consistent in your actions and words. You should continually demonstrate your love for her. As much as humanly possible, you need to "Be Nice" and you must attempt to consistently stay nice. At present, there is a possibility that the main thing your wife is looking for is evidence that proves you will ultimately disappoint her.

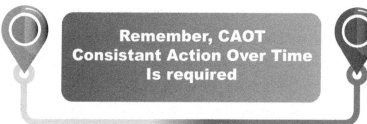

Remember, CAOT
Consistant Action Over Time
Is required

At this time, I would encourage you to prayerfully seek to stay strong. Don't let your actions or words to your wife be based on your wife. Let me reiterate this, "Who you are cannot be determined by your wife!" How she acts cannot influence how you act towards her. How she talks to you cannot influence how you talk to her. You might be wondering, "How is this possible?" It is only possible as your focus stays steady on being the husband God wants you to be. Ultimately this is what matters most.

I have known a host of men who are very strong with their words about their intent to be Godly husbands. However, with one harsh comment or gesture from their wife, they react poorly. How are you? Are you one look, one negative comment about your hunting dog, one innuendo about your sports activities, one statement about your work schedule, one rejection of your sexual advance ...and there you go, showing yourself to be far less of a man than the husband you should be to your wife.

STAND FIRM

Focus on being accountable to God for the husband you are to your wife...for words spoken, for action taken. See yourself as standing before God. Don't use your wife as an excuse for being anyone less than the husband God is calling you to be. You cannot pull an Adam. Remember how Adam blamed his wife and God, for the reason he had made certain bad choices. In Genesis 3:12 Adam said, "The woman you put here with me—she gave me some fruit from the tree, and I ate it."

No Excuses ... BE THE MAN!

BE GOD'S MAN!

1 Corinthians 16:13 "Be on the alert, stand firm in the faith, act like men, be strong."

REMEMBER

As you pray for God's strength to enable you, stand before God as a man solely accountable TO HIM for your words and actions to your wife, as you seek to be a husband honoring in God's sight.

Chapter 14
Hold Fast . . . The Moments

Life's moments can be a lot more enjoyable when you have someone by your side. Maybe God was referencing that fact when He said, "It is not good for man to be alone" (Genesis 2:18).

FROM FIRST MOMENTS TO NOW

During the first few years of our marriage, Joyce and I did not do very well with the moments we shared together. I typically tell young couples that Joyce and I had some horrible first years. I want them to know that everything is not always wonderful, so they will not be surprised when marriage is not too fun.

Now I am not sure why Joyce and I had such a rough time. I am a nice person and Joyce is really nice. Apparently, you can take two really nice people, and still end up with some really miserable moments together.

I was a minister in a church, and in some ways, I believe that too often in those first few years I took the best of myself outside the home and brought back my leftovers. You may understand. I would leave home in the morning, showered, shaved, well rested and smelling good. I would come home late, sweaty and tired, with my shirt tail hanging out (when exposed shirt tails were considered unkept). I would go from "Got Game" as I walked out the door in the morning, to "Got Nothing," when I arrived back home in the evening. However, Joyce and I really were both nice but maybe we were so nice to everyone else that when we arrived back home, we took for granted the importance of being nice to one another. Several years into our journey we finally learned the importance of two nice and kindhearted people like ourselves, actually being nice to one another. Somewhere along the way, our "marriage moments," became the cherished moments of my life.

The last few years for Joyce and me have not been easy. There has been a mixture of intense sorrow and great joy. It is not a matter of Joyce and me struggling in our relationship with each other. She has continued to be really nice to me. I have done my best to be careful with our moments together and to be nice to her. There is never a day I do not tell her I love her. I tell her how pretty she is numerous times a day. She sometimes tells others that I treat her as if every day is her birthday, and every day is her wedding anniversary. I hope she always feels that way.

Sometimes at night, I will wake her up and ask her if I can hold her. It probably sounds horrible that I wake her up, but I just don't want to waste too many moments. And so I ask, "Can I hold you?" After which she usually turns to me and rests her head on my shoulder, and I wrap my arms around her. I will listen to her breathe. I will often stroke her hair gently with my hand.

As you and I have talked in previous chapters, as husbands we need to transform as many moments as possible. Of course, I would guess there are some nights after I wake Joyce up, she is wishing I had left that moment alone.

Four years ago, Joyce and I began a journey with cancer. It started in Joyce's breast. Some of you know that path as well. After surgery, chemo, and radiation, we had hoped the journey had concluded. Nonetheless, a year later a tumor started growing in Joyce's hip. Her oncologist was confident it was nothing. I could write on, but the bottom line, it was a rare and aggressive cancer that in a matter of 3 months grew from 1 cm to 9.3 cm in size. There was a surgery in Atlanta, another surgery at MD Anderson in Houston, and a month of radiation treatments in Houston. Joyce is doing great now. However, the events of the past four years have continually reminded me that we live in the frailty of a body that has limited moments. Even though I had always known of the frailty of our bodies, our journey with cancer has heightened my awareness of our frailties. It makes me more careful with our moments together. Perspective is a powerful teacher.

JUST FIVE MORE MINUTES

In closing our time together, I want to share with you an event that is very personal to me. I share it with you in the hopes it will be as meaningful to you as it has been to me.

Several years ago, I walked into the room where Joyce's dad was resting. Joyce's mom was seated at his bedside. (Sadly, Joyce's dad was suffering with cancer. He would die three days later.) As I walked into the room, Joyce's mom was singing to Joyce's dad and rubbing his hands with lotion. The song that Joyce's mom was singing was "Always." It was their song, the song that was sung at their wedding some 60 years earlier.

The words of the chorus that Joyce's mom was singing were:

Days may not be fair always,
That's when I'll be there always.
Not for just an hour,
Not for just a day,
Not for just a year,
But always.

When Joyce's mom saw me, she said, "Oh you've caught us making love." (And in so many ways I think we often miss out on what real love looks like.) She continued . . . "He always liked for his skin to look nice." And looking down at her hands which were crippled with arthritis she said, "I was just so tired after putting the lotion on him, I just didn't have the strength to put it on me." That is Love.

Thomas Carlyle, has written what has been termed the saddest sentence in the English Language when after the death of his wife he wrote, "Oh, that I had you yet for five minutes by my side, that I might tell you all."

There will probably be a moment in many of our lives when we would give everything we have for just five more minutes with the precious person who sleeps by our side... Just Five More Minutes. Today, let us not waste the minutes, ...the moments that God gives us.

As warriors, as men of God, let us transform the moments of our lives.

As I am writing this, it is very late. Joyce is in our bed asleep. I think I will go wake her up.

MORE TO COME

In the coming days I will release the wive's editon of *Guide to a Good Marriage*. This book will be quite similar to the book you hold in your hand (so you can just let your wife read this book) with a few changes that are directed solely to women.

In addition to *Guide to a Good Marriage for Christian Wives*, Joyce and I are writing a book entitled, *A Guide to a Good Marriage: Sex and the Christian Couple*. For many years Joyce and I taught a variety of "sex" workshops for Lifeway, with such titles as: Celebrating Sex in Marriage, From Good Sex to Great Sex, and Was That As Good For You.

During these conferences we often surveyed conference participants. *A Guide to a Good Marriage: Sex and the Christian Couple* will draw from workshop presentations and the survey responses. It is some great material and I think you will find the results gathered from years of participant responses quite interesting.

WANT TO STAY IN TOUCH?

Sign up at HelpIAmMarried.com to be the first to know about new books and other projects from Dr. Dan McKay and Joyce McKay, Ed.S

Made in United States
Orlando, FL
16 October 2023